Start Your Own

CONSULTING

BUSINESS

Additional titles in *Entrepreneur's* **Startup Series**

Start Your Own

Entrepreneur
MAGAZINE'S

start*up*

2ND EDITION

Start Your Own

CONSULTING BUSINESS

*Your Step-by-Step
Guide to Success*

Entrepreneur Press and Eileen Sandlin

EP
Entrepreneur
Press

Editorial Director: Jere L. Calmes
Managing Editor: Marla Markman
Cover Design: Beth Hansen-Winter
Production: Eliot House Productions
Composition: Tricia Miller

This publication is designed to provide accurate and authoritative information in regard to the subject matter covered. It is sold with the understanding that the publisher is not engaged in rendering legal, accounting or other professional services. If legal advice or other expert assistance is required, the services of a competent professional person should be sought.

Library of Congress Cataloging-in-Publication Data

Sandlin, Eileen Figure.
    Start your own consulting business/by Eileen Figure Sandlin.—2nd ed.
        p.   cm.
    Rev. of: Entrepreneur magazine's consulting business/John Riddle.
    ISBN-10: 1-59918-048-0 (alk. paper)
    ISBN-13: 978-159918048-9
        1. Business consultants. 2. Career changes. 3. Entrepreneurship. 4. New business enterprises—Management. I. Riddle, John. Entrepreneur magazine's consulting business. II. Entrepreneur Press. III. Title.
    HD69.C6R535 2006
    001—dc22   2006021894

Printed in Canada

12 11 10 09 08 07   10 9 8 7 6 5 4 3 2

Contents

Preface

If you've been dreaming of leaving your current job to become the chief executive of your own small business, you've retired and want to put your knowledge and talents to work in a new business, or you just want to earn some extra money on the side, then you've come to the right place. The book you're holding is your personal roadmap to becoming a self-employed entrepreneur in your own consulting business. It touches on all of the ground work you'll need to do, from selecting a business name, to obtaining business licenses, drumming up work, wrangling financing, and more—tasks that are just as necessary for success as your talents and skills will be when you finally hang out your shingle on that first day on the job.

And that day could be pretty scary. After all, you won't be getting a paycheck the following Friday. You won't have coworkers to commiserate with, or a support staff to cater to your every whim. In fact, possibly for the first time you'll be handling tasks you've never done before, like one consultant we know, who said, "I ran a corporate business, but a lot of things were done automatically for me. I didn't truly understand [things like] profit and loss statements versus cash flow statements because I had financial people who worried about those things for me."

We can help. This book contains information on the major tasks you'll encounter on the road to successful self-employment, including the 411 you need on:

- Assessing your skills and defining your market
- Selecting a legal form of operation and naming your business
- Finding business professionals to help run the show
- Setting up your home office
- Managing daily administrative tasks
- Hiring personnel (something that could happen sooner than you think)
- Locating professional development resources
- Prospecting for clients and promoting your business
- Establishing an internet presence
- Financing the business and staying in the black
- And much more

So no matter whether your consulting business will focus on human resources placement, computer troubleshooting, public relations, meeting planning, or anything else you can dream up, you're about to join the other 10.5 million people in the United States who have decided to seek their fame and fortune armed only with their own talents, capabilities, ambition, and determination.

Enjoy the ride.

The Right
Stuff

What is a consultant? The dictionary defines a consultant as "an expert in a particular field who works as an advisor either to a company or to another individual." Sounds pretty vague, doesn't it? But unless you've been in a coma for the past decade, you probably have a good idea what a consultant is.

Businesses certainly understand what consultants are and what their value is. According to the online statistical source Biz-Stats.com, U.S. businesses spent nearly $28 billion on consulting services in 2003, while Plunkett Research Ltd. reports that worldwide consulting revenues were $115 billion. And since at least 60 percent of all businesses use independent contractors such as consultants (according to the Bureau of Labor Statistics), you can see that the market is wide open for new consultants in virtually every industry.

And there's more good news. The U.S. Department of Labor's *Occupational Outlook Handbook 2004-05 Edition* says:

- The consulting industry ranks among the fastest growing through the year 2012.
- The industry is one of the highest paying around.
- The industry's workers are highly educated (72 percent have a bachelor's degree or higher).

But why exactly are consultants in such high demand? First, companies understand the value consultants bring to their organizations by virtue of their experience, expertise, and knowledge. Second, consultants bring fresh ideas and a fresh perspective to projects. And third, companies that have to lay off workers for economic reasons still need to get the work done despite their reduced labor pools.

Taking the Plunge

For their part, independent consultants have different motivations for taking the plunge into self-employment. Some of them are baby boomers who may have worked for years—or decades—for one or more companies, and simply are ready for a career that will allow them to call the shots for a change. Others, like Bill Metten, a consultant in Hockessin, Delaware, have been laid off or downsized out of a job and decide to seek a new opportunity that will allow them to use the knowledge they've acquired on the job.

"I was a senior executive for a chemical company when the industry went to pot in the early 1990s," says Metten, who founded his public relations/customer service consultant business in 1991. "The company made me an offer I couldn't refuse, and since I had long harbored the desire to have just a few clients and spoil the dickens out of them, I decided to take the plunge."

And still others, like Melinda Patrician, a public relations consultant in Arlington,

Smart Tip
Before you decide on a consulting specialty, make sure you have a passion for that field. If you can imagine talking with someone for hours at a time about your specialty without referring to notes or books, then you clearly have selected the right field in which to work as a consultant.

Virginia, discovered that technology has made it easier to work as a consultant from home.

"The same technology that has helped me to be successful as a consultant has made it easier for others to do the same," Patrician says.

Simply put, a consultant's job is to consult. It's that simple. But what separates a good consultant from a bad consultant is a passion and drive for excellence. And—oh yes—good consultants should be knowledgeable about the subjects they are consulting in.

Beware!
If you decide to do consulting in more than one field, be certain that you can devote enough time and energy to both; otherwise, you run the risk of having both of your consulting specialties fail.

You see, in this day and age, anyone can be a consultant, and you can be a consultant in pretty much any field or discipline, from management to wedding coordination, academic course design, interior design, and much more. All you need to discover is what your particular gift is. For example, are you very comfortable working around computers? Do you keep up with the latest software and hardware information, which seems to be changing almost daily? And are you able to take that knowledge you have gained and turn it into a resource that someone would be willing to pay money for? Then you would have no trouble working as a computer consultant.

Or maybe you're an expert in the fundraising field. Maybe you have worked for nonprofit agencies in marketing, public relations, or sales, and over the years you have discovered how to raise money. It's possible to turn fundraising successes into a lucrative consulting business, according to John Riddle, a fundraising consultant in Bear, Delaware, who has done just that.

Fundraising is growing in small social services agencies, such as soup kitchens and homeless shelters, and in large universities, colleges, and nonprofit hospitals. Once you have successfully learned how to write grant proposals to foundations and corporations and get a few years of experience under your belt, there's no reason you shouldn't be joining the ranks of fundraising consultants who are earning six figures—and more.

Smart Tip
Tip...
Develop your own short- and long-term goals, and put them down on paper. Revise them as often as necessary. By having your goals written down, you will be more likely to meet them.

And in case you are wondering, yes, it is possible to be a consultant in more than one field at the same time. Riddle did this when, in addition to having built a successful fundraising consulting business, he simultaneously used his gift of writing to develop an editorial consulting business. It wasn't unusual for Riddle to find himself meeting with the board of directors of a nonprofit agency concerning fundraising strategies one day, and the next day showing a client how to break into the publishing world by writing book reviews for his or her local newspaper. He confesses, however, that at times he wished he had concentrated on one or the other field and not felt so compelled to work in different areas. Certainly that's good advice for someone in the fledgling stages of establishing a consulting business.

Things to Consider

When it comes right down to it, working as a consultant can be very exciting and lucrative. Where else can you work as a self-employed independent agent, set your own hours, and even set your own fees? Of course, you must be willing to devote the time and effort it takes to make a living as a consultant; otherwise, your consulting

---

'Tis the Reason

Although money is sometimes a key factor when someone decides to become a consultant, there are a few other reasons why people choose this profession:

- ○ *You are not living your dream.* Maybe your dream has been to work on your own and to be your own boss. As a consultant, you are responsible for your career, not someone else's.

- ○ *You are about to lose your job (or have already).* Job security is almost a thing of the past, as everyone knows. Gone are the days when you work for the same company for 20 to 30 years, receive your gold watch, and spend your retirement fishing. As a consultant, you have the power to control your economic future—and ultimate happiness.

- ○ *You have a talent people will pay money for.* Suppose that for 20 years you learned how to raise money for nonprofit organizations, and during that time you built quite a reputation for yourself. Odds are, people will pay you for your talent.

- ○ *You want an additional source of income.* Maybe your goal or desire is to work only part time as a consultant. Many consultants in this country are successfully supplementing their incomes by practicing on the side. Be advised, however, if your consulting business begins to interfere with your main job, you may have to choose between the two.

- ○ *You believe you can make a difference.* Many people become consultants simply because they know they can do a particular job better than someone else. If you believe in something, nothing should stand in your way!

business will be doomed to fail even before it gets off the ground.

Consulting is not for the faint of heart, says Huntington Beach, California, human resources consultant Susan Bock, who is also president of the Association of Professional Consultants. "This is not the business arena for someone who enjoys predictability," she says. "There are no two days or months that are exactly the same, which can be intimidating for some people. But

> **Bright Idea**
> Make a list of the top 10 reasons why a business should hire you as a consultant. This will help you when you prepare your marketing strategy and pitch your services to clients.

for someone who loves the freedom of working with his or her own clients, it's a wonderful life, and one that allows for exponential personal and professional growth."

When considering starting a consulting business, first ask yourself: What certifications and special licensing will I need? Depending upon your profession, you may need special certification or a special license before you can begin operating as a consultant. For example, fundraising consultants do not need special certification, although you can become certified through the Association of Fund Raising Professionals. And in some states, you may need to register as a professional fundraising consultant before starting your business.

- *Am I qualified to become a consultant?* Before you hang out your shingle and hope that clients will begin beating down your door to hire you, make sure you have the qualifications necessary to get the job done. If you want to be a computer consultant, for example, make sure you are up-to-date in the knowledge department with all the trends and changes in the computer industry.
- *Am I organized enough to become a consultant?* Do I like to plan my day? Am I an expert when it comes to time management? You should have answered "yes" to all three of those questions!
- *Do I like to network?* Networking is critical to the success of any type of consultant today. Begin building your network of contacts immediately.
- *Have I set long- and short-term goals?* Do they allow for me to become a consultant? If your goals do not match up with the time and energy it takes to open and successfully build a consulting business, then reconsider before making any move in this direction.

Do You Have What It Takes?

While just about anybody can be a consultant, the best ones possess some important skills, including:

- *Listening skills.* When people talk, do you listen? This may sound like a dumb question, but listening is an acquired skill. By carefully listening to your clients' needs, you will better be able to solve their problems.

- *Investigative skills.* You need to have the ability to investigate and uncover the data necessary to complete your consulting assignment. In time, your investigative skills will become fine tuned.

- *Analytical skills.* When you investigate and uncover data, you had better know what it means! Your ability to understand and analyze complex information relative to your consulting field is paramount to success.

- *Change skills.* No, we don't mean exact change for the bus! You must be a person who embraces change and who can persuade your clients to make the changes necessary to solve their problems.

- *Action skills.* A good consultant will be ready to "take the bull by the horns" and do whatever it takes to get the job done. In other words, you will take action with a capital "A."

You'll learn more about the day-to-day responsibilities of running a consulting business in Chapter 3.

A Brief History of Consulting

It wasn't until the 1950s that consultants began to emerge in the business world. Until then, consultants could be found in the legal, finance, and employment fields. Then something happened. When the U.S. economy changed from production- to service-oriented in the early 1960s, the real birth of the consulting industry took place. Since most consultants were providing a service as experts in a particular field, they were welcomed with open arms by both large and small businesses throughout the land.

Then during the economic recession of the late 1970s and early 1980s, corporate America suddenly found it difficult to turn a profit. There seemed to be no other way to boost the bottom line than by reducing staff. So little by little, businesses began to cut back on operating costs by offering early retirement packages to long-term employees and laying off anyone they felt was expendable.

From a corporate point of view, the thinking was simply "It makes sense to hire a consultant," since paying a consultant seemed like a cost-effective means of doing business. So not only was there a boost in the demand for consultants, but also many people who had accepted early retirement packages were now setting up shop as consultants, often working for the very businesses that had let them go.

At the same time, many consultants were faced with a dilemma most people never have to face: Too much business! So rather than turn away a client, independent consultants joined with other consultants in their field, and thus the consulting industry was born.

According to industry experts, here are the top ten reasons organizations hire consultants:

Beware!
Before accepting any consulting assignment, be certain that the potential client is not involved in any litigation concerning employment discrimination practices.

1. *A consultant may be hired because of his or her expertise.* This is where it pays not only to be really good in your chosen field, but also to have some type of track record that speaks for itself. For example, Riddle says he knows that every client who hired him did so partly on the basis of his track record. After all, if you are a nonprofit organization that needs to raise $1 million, it makes sense to hire someone who has already raised millions for other organizations.

2. *A consultant may be hired to identify problems.* Sometimes employees are too close to a problem inside an organization to identify it. That's when a consultant rides in on his or her white horse to save the day.

3. *A consultant may be hired to supplement the staff.* Sometimes a business discovers it can save thousands of dollars a week by hiring consultants when they are needed rather than hiring full-time employees. Businesses realize they save additional money by not having to pay benefits for consultants they hire. Even though a consultant's fees are generally higher than an employee's salary, over the long haul it simply makes good economic sense to hire a consultant.

4. *A consultant may be hired to act as a catalyst.* No one likes change, especially corporate America. But sometimes change is needed, and a consultant may be brought in to "get the ball rolling." In other words, the consultant can do things without worrying about the corporate culture, employee morale, or other issues that get in the way when an organization is trying to institute change.

5. *A consultant may be hired to provide much-needed objectivity.* Who else is more qualified to identify a problem than a consultant? A good consultant provides an objective, fresh viewpoint—without worrying about what people in the organization might think about the results and how they were achieved.

6. *A consultant may be hired to teach.* These days if you are a computer consultant who can show employees how to master a new program, then your telephone probably hasn't stopped ringing for a while. A consultant may be asked to teach employees any number of different skills. However, consultants must be willing to keep up with new discoveries in their field of expertise—and be ready to teach new clients what they need to stay competitive.

7. *A consultant may be hired to do the "dirty work."* Let's face it: No one wants to be the person who has to make cuts in the staff or to eliminate an entire division.

8. *A consultant may be hired to bring new life to an organization.* If you are good at coming up with new ideas that work, then you won't have any trouble finding clients. At one time or another, most businesses need someone to administer "first aid" to get things rolling again.

9. *A consultant may be hired to create a new business.* There are consultants who have become experts in this field. Keep in mind, however, that not everyone has the ability to conceive an idea and develop a game plan.

10. *A consultant may be hired to influence other people.* Do you like to hang out with the rich and famous in your town? If so, you may be hired to do a consulting job simply based on who you know.

The Top Consulting Businesses

Although you can be a consultant in just about any field these days, the top types of consulting businesses that are thriving today, according to the Association of Professional Consultants, are:

- *Accounting.* Accounting is something that every business needs, no matter how large or small. Accounting consultants can help a business with all its financial needs.

- *Advertising.* With the price of advertising these days, it's no wonder that anyone with any type of advertising expertise can earn a good living as an advertising consultant. This type of consultant is normally hired by a business to develop good strategic advertising campaigns.

- *Auditing.* From consultants who audit utility bills for small businesses to consultants who handle major work for telecommunications firms, auditing consultants are enjoying the fruits of their labor. This type of consultant is normally hired to audit various utility bills for corporations.

Quittin' Time

Before you decide to open up shop, think carefully about why you want to become a consultant. It's important that you don't become a consultant for all the wrong reasons. For example, if you and your boss are not getting along, but you have had differences with him or her in the past and have always reached an understanding, then you probably don't want to leave your job and become a consultant. However, if you are really dissatisfied with your boss and your company and can envision doing the work more efficiently on your own, then you are probably starting a consulting business for all the right reasons.

- *Business.* Know how to help a business turn a profit? If you have good business sense, then you'll do well as a business consultant. After computer consulting, people in this field are the most sought after.

- *Business writing.* Everyone knows that most businesspeople have trouble when it comes to writing a report—or even a simple memo. Enter the business writing consultant, and everyone is happy!

- *Communications.* A good communications consultant will never have to worry about where his or her next meal is coming from. Communications consultants specialize in helping employees in large and small businesses communicate better with each other, which ultimately makes the business more efficient and operate smoothly.

- *Computer consulting.* From software to hardware and everything in between, if you know computers, your biggest problem will be not having enough hours in the day to meet your clients' demands!

- *Editorial services.* From producing newsletters to corporate annual reports, consultants who are experts in the editorial field will always be appreciated.

- *Grantsmanship.* Once you learn how to write a grant proposal, you can name your price.

- *Human resources.* As long as businesses have people problems (and they always will), consultants in this field will enjoy a never-ending supply of corporate clients, both large and small. People-problem prevention programs could include teaching employees to get along with others, respect each other, and even prevent violence in the workplace.

- *Insurance.* Everyone needs insurance, and everyone needs an insurance consultant to help them find the best plan and pricing for them.

- *Marketing.* Can you help a business write a marketing plan? Or do you have ideas that you feel will help promote a business? If so, why not try your hand as a marketing consultant?

- *Payroll management.* Everyone needs to get paid. By using your knowledge and expertise in payroll management, you can provide this service to many businesses, both large and small.

- *Public relations.* Getting good press coverage for any organization is a real art. When an organization finds a good PR consultant, they hang on to him or her for life!

- *Publishing.* If you are interested in the publishing field, then learn everything you can and you, too, can be a publishing consultant. A publishing consultant usually helps new ventures when they are ready to launch a new newspaper, magazine, newsletter—and even web sites and electronic newsletters.

- *Taxes.* With the right marketing and business plan (and a sincere interest in taxes), your career as a tax consultant can be very lucrative. A tax consultant advises businesses on the legal ways to pay the least amount of tax possible.

- *Writing services.* Anything related to the written word will always be in demand. Find your specialty in the writing field, and the sky will be the limit!

What's Your
Specialty?

To be a really successful consultant, you need to be working in a field in which you are an expert. You see, working as a consultant is different from going to work as an employee. Every day in this country, millions of people go to work. Most of them are probably not happy with their jobs for one reason or another. It may be due to low pay or a long commute, or it may be they just don't get along with their bosses. This chapter will help you take a look at what you're really good at, which you just may be able to turn into a successful consulting business.

Expert Advice

More than 20 years ago, John Riddle was one of those unhappy employees. He went to work every day, hated his job, despised the corporate culture, and generally was not a happy camper. At the time, he was working in the payroll department of a large chemical company in Delaware. Although he was good at the job he was doing, his true passion was not handling the payroll and the endless reports the department had to produce.

Bright Idea

Do you have a hobby you're passionate about? You might be able to turn it into a successful consulting business. If you collect antiques, for example, you could use your knowledge of the antiques industry to provide appraisal services.

Instead, Riddle's true passion was writing. And even though he had no real experience as a writer, he had read nearly every book that had been written about how to make it as a writer. So after seven years in the payroll department, he left the company and went to work for a small public relations firm, where he was able to do some promotional writing and event planning.

It didn't matter to Riddle that he had taken a pay cut, or that job security was no longer a benefit. He was working in his true passion area. He was a writer! And within a few years, he had written several books and had started selling newspaper and magazine articles to publications throughout the country. He had found happiness and contentment, all because he was doing something he truly enjoyed. It was no longer "Thank God it's Friday," but "Thank God it's Monday."

So do you know what your field of expertise is? What subject can you talk about for hours at a time without worrying about how long you have been talking? Now, don't confuse something you do in your spare time with a field of expertise. Be certain there is a market for your chosen consulting field. If you choose a specialty so obscure that you have no clients, then obviously you'll have no business.

Smart Tip

Tip...

Since the consulting business is all about people, use every opportunity available to develop a relationship with the people you are working for. Be someone they will come to depend on now and in the future.

Newark, Delaware, consultant Merrily Schiavone never had a problem drumming up business because she was able to parlay her expertise as a newspaper advertising salesperson into a new career as a consultant. She found herself giving advice to her newspaper clients on how to market their business better, and since she also had a background in graphic arts, it was a natural jump into full-time consulting.

"I actually started getting clients while I was selling newspaper ad space, and I quickly realized that was a conflict of interest," Schiavone explains. "So I started a one-person advertising agency."

As mentioned earlier, Riddle discovered that one of his true passions is writing. Not only has the Bear, Delaware, consultant been published in a variety of media over the past 20 years, he also has taught workshops and published newsletters to show people how to break into the wonderful world of freelance writing. When he presents workshops, it's not unusual for him to end up staying an hour or so afterwards just to answer questions or to help someone who is not quite sure if he or she understands what must be done to become a freelance writer. Riddle connects with his students not only because he's passionate about the subject, but also because he knows what it's like to get that first article published in a newspaper or a magazine—basically you're busting out all over with happiness.

Assessing Your Skills and Talents

If you want a career as a consultant, you should be aware of both your strengths and weaknesses and how relevant they are to this type of work. While you may already know—or think you know—what type of consulting field you want to break into, it really is a good idea to take some time to assess your skills and talents. Remember the discussion about how Riddle had worked in the payroll department for seven years but wasn't really happy? Well, even though he did not like his job, he was good at what he had to accomplish each day. And like any other job, it got easier—and he learned how

Quality Check

Do you have what it takes to succeed as a consultant? Check out the top ten qualities every good consultant possesses:

1. Intelligence
2. Flexibility
3. Critical thinking skills
4. Reliability
5. Resourcefulness
6. Excellent communication skills
7. Integrity
8. Perseverance
9. Sense of humor
10. Dedication

to do it better as time passed. Riddle was skilled and talented in the area of payroll and finances, which served him well when he ultimately became a fundraising consultant.

For years, career counseling consultants have been advising their clients to make a list of what they feel they excel at and compare that to a list of things they would rather spend their day doing. Sometimes people have talents in areas they weren't ever aware of. For example, a young mother who has made the decision to stay at home with her children has had to master the fine arts of time management (scheduling time for her, the children, and her husband), budgeting (paying bills, banking, and money management), and even negotiation. (Ever try to get two children to agree with each other? It's not easy!) Without realizing it, she's been developing the skills essential to being a professional consultant.

Take a look at the Skills and Talent Worksheet on page 15. After you have answered those questions, make a list of the things you can do (with regard to your potential consulting career). And at the same time, make a list of things that you would rather be doing. Remember, there are no right or wrong answers!

Your list might look something like this:

- Things I can do: typing, special event planning, teaching, researching, writing, editing, sales, public relations, and promotions
- Things I would rather be doing: collecting big, fat royalty checks, writing, dancing, teaching writing workshops, watching television, and going to the movies

You may not have guessed that some items will appear on both lists. And when you come across such items, then you have discovered one way of finding out how to turn your true passions into a successful consulting business.

So as you prepare to launch your consulting career, don't forget to do some real soul searching and select a field in which you will really excel. One thing you shouldn't do, however, is attempt to be all things to all people. And you will be tempted, especially in the early days of your new career.

"This is a struggle every emerging consultant faces," says Huntington Beach, California, human resources consultant Susan Bock. "Being desperate for success, new consultants tend to say 'yes' to everything. But this is the biggest disservice you can do to yourself. Always be very clear about what you can and want to do, and the business will come."

Once you've assessed your skills and selected a field, be sure that what you are proposing to do for a client will make a difference for them. If you're not sure if you can make a difference, ask yourself these five questions:

1. Am I confident I can solve a client's problem?

2. Am I confident I can find new and creative solutions to these problems?

3. Am I confident I can meet the deadlines and work in almost any environment?

4. Am I confident I can work within the budget presented by the client?

5. Am I confident I can repeat steps 1 through 4 every day?

Skills and Talents Worksheet

If you don't acknowledge your hidden skills and talents, you will never be able to present them to your clients—and make a living at the same time. So grab a pencil and get ready to work.

○ What job skills do you possess that are really outstanding?

_____

_____

_____

○ What specialized training or education do you have?

_____

_____

_____

○ What do you like the most about your present job or occupation?

_____

_____

_____

○ What special license(s) do you possess in your present job?

_____

_____

_____

○ What have you been told that you do extremely well?

_____

_____

_____

Defining Your Market

You've determined that you have the experience and you've got something to offer. It's time to get serious about your chosen consulting field. By now you have learned that you need to be excited, interested, passionate, and expert in whatever it is you have chosen to consult about. But there is one more very important feature to consider: Your idea may be the best one you have ever thought of, but there needs to be a market for that idea. In other words, someone must be willing and able to pay you for your expert advice.

Outstanding in the Field

If you want your earnings to be in the six-figure range, you need to become an outstanding consultant, not a mediocre one. What makes the difference? The best consultants all practice the following:

○ Eat, drink, and breathe customer service. If you do not live by the creed of "giving more than you have," you won't be remembered as a consultant who goes the extra mile for customers.

○ Keep up with the latest changes in your field of expertise. Read professional journals, attend workshops, and network with other people in your field.

○ Develop the ability to identify problems quickly. Know what you're talking about. Clients hire you because of your expertise; don't disappoint them.

○ Look for creative ways to solve problems. Put on your thinking cap!

○ Use excellent communication skills. Read, attend workshops, practice writing reports—whatever it takes to enhance your ability to communicate.

○ Be 100 percent confident that you will succeed. Everyone likes to work with people who are certain that everything they undertake will be a success.

○ Be professional in everything you do. (This had better not warrant further explanation; otherwise, you may want to reconsider your decision to get into the consulting business!)

○ Be a people person. It takes a real "people person" to be a successful consultant. How are your people skills?

○ Be ready, willing, and able to be the best manager you can be. Good managers are experts at time management and doing whatever it takes to get the job done.

○ Give your clients more than they expect. You'll be surprised at their responses.

Just who is your target audience? In other words, who are your potential clients? Will you be marketing your consulting services to large corporations? Or will you offer a specialty that would be of interest only to smaller businesses? Perhaps your services will be sought after by nonprofit organizations. Whatever the case, before you go forward, make sure you spend time preparing both a business and a marketing plan. You won't be disappointed with the results—especially when clients begin paying you!

Bright Idea

Take a few minutes and brainstorm who you think your first 10 clients would be. Is this list easy for you to develop? If so, you have the right attitude. If the list is difficult to produce, rethink why you are getting into the consulting business.

Bock is one consultant who realized early on that she preferred working with smaller companies, and as a result targeted her efforts toward only that type of business.

"Working with larger organizations is like trying to turn the Titanic," she says. "Smaller companies—and especially women-owned companies—appealed to me because I can understand and appreciate the issues of both small businesses and women. I also like immediate gratification, which you can't get working with a big company."

The best answer to the question, "Who are the people who will pay for your services?" is simply this: anyone who has a need you can fill! As a case in point, a few years ago, Riddle almost lost a consulting client. A local nonprofit theater group was looking for a fundraising consultant to design a plan and raise a little more than half a million dollars so they could make some improvements to their building. They had narrowed their search down to another consultant and him. Because they were probably equally qualified, it was difficult for them to choose one over another. So they called both back in for a few more interview questions.

Riddle arrived early and sat outside the boardroom waiting patiently for his turn. Much to his surprise, he was able to hear what was taking place inside that room. The other candidate was busy talking about what contacts he had made in the entertainment industry, including the theatrical world. He was dropping names that no doubt impressed the search committee.

Well, right then and there Riddle knew he had two choices. Number one, he could come up with his own list of celebrity contacts (since he had done a fair number of celebrity interviews as a freelance writer) and try to dazzle the search

Bright Idea

Consider sending a survey to a variety of organizations you would like to have as clients. In your survey, ask if they have ever worked with a consultant in the past and ask them to share as much fee information as they can. And don't forget to ask them if they were pleased with the consultant's performance, and if they felt they received their money's worth.

committee. Or his second choice was to simply reiterate what he could do for them: He could raise the money they needed within the time frame they had come up with. Period. Nothing more, nothing less.

Guess who got the job?

Figuring out who you will be trying to solicit as clients doesn't involve a complicated formula. The best place to start is to seek out potential clients in your chosen field of expertise. For example, if, like Riddle, you decide to become a fundraising consultant, check to see what nonprofit organizations in your town need to raise money but don't know how to go about putting a fundraising plan into action.

How do you go about finding those potential clients? There are plenty of free resources available to help you create a list, including the phone book, the local chamber of commerce directory, the daily newspaper, a network of friends, and so on. Chapters 9 and 10 cover this in more detail.

Consulting
Basics

As we mentioned in Chapter 1, it's possible to consult in virtually any field, no matter whether it is technical or nontechnical. Although the issues and problems you'll consult on will vary depending on your specialty (such as engineering, information technology, human resources, strategic planning, and so on), some aspects of running a consulting business are pretty much the same no matter what your expertise is. This chapter will cover some of the day-to-day functions involved in managing a small consulting practice as well as strategies for providing excellent customer service.

A Day in the Life

Consultants have three basic functions: to advise clients, to implement solutions, and to teach clients how to do business better in some way. But the life of a consultant consists of much more than this. While it's likely no two days will be the same, you will find there are certain professional and administrative tasks you'll do on a regular basis. For instance, you'll have to prospect for clients and attend to the administrative tasks necessary to keep a small business running. On a typical day, you'll be on the phone making cold calls. You'll attend meetings of local associations and/or service groups so you can network for future business. You'll write proposals to persuade prospective clients to hire you over the competition, and later you'll negotiate contracts detailing your responsibilities. You'll also be called on to give quotes that estimate how much your services will cost for specific projects. Then when you do win a contract, you'll spend time mulling over solutions to the proposed problem, then writing a comprehensive report outlining the solutions. (You'll find a sample report in Chapter 13.)

Monotony is one thing you won't find in the consulting business: "And I like it that way. I like the variety," says Huntington Beach, California, human resources consultant Susan Bock.

Merrily Schiavone finds herself doing a tremendous amount of e-mailing to keep her Newark, Delaware, advertising consulting business running. "It's an efficient way to make contacts early in the day, especially since I'm an owl, not a lark, and I prefer to spend the afternoon and evenings doing the creative stuff," she says.

General office administration duties will also include spending time on the telephone every day fielding inquiries from interested clients and keeping up with paperwork, such as incoming mail and outgoing tax payments (since self-employed people may be required to make quarterly estimated tax payments). You most likely will handle your own invoicing and track your receivables (although we'll discuss

Bright Idea
Keep up with the business books published each year. Some of the information will no doubt be helpful to you and your clients.

Smart Tip
Tip...
You don't have to be an expert at time management to have a career as a consultant—unless you want to cash a lot of checks in a given year. In other words, you need to get organized and manage your time well if you want to be a successful consultant.

how an accountant can help with the financial side of your business in Chapter 5). You'll also be in charge of paying any bills incurred by the business, advertising your services, and overseeing the work of any employees you decide to hire.

Providing Excellent Customer Service

To make it as a consultant, do everything you can to set yourself apart from the competition. You want to give your clients a reason to say "We're really glad we chose this consultant." In other words, you want your clients to be happy at every stage of the relationship.

One way to ensure that the relationship stays happy is to provide the best customer service on the planet. The best way to do this is by communicating with your client often about whether his or her expectations are being met and the project is progressing as desired.

"At the end of the first month of a project, I always ask my clients whether they think value is being achieved," says Bock, "and I'll give them a full refund and won't proceed any further if I determine it's not possible to deal with their unrealized expectations."

Another example of outstanding customer service comes from Stew Leonard, an entrepreneur who owns a store in Norwalk, Connecticut, that's billed as "The World's Largest Dairy." His store, Stew Leonard's, combines elements of Disneyland and Dale Carnegie, and it delivers a straightforward message: Have fun!

In his case, fun equals big-time profits—a few years ago, Stew Leonard was grossing more than $150 million annually, making his store the most successful supermarket in the country. Customers go out of their way to shop there, and they all agree that the reason they shop there is because it is fun. Fun is just the tip of the iceberg, however; Leonard's success rests on his scrupulous management and marketing practices, plus a devotion to customer service that borders on the fanatical. As a result, he has won the praise of *Fortune* 500 executives and has been cited by author Tom Peters in his book *In Search of Excellence* (Warner Books, 1988).

To understand what his customers want, Leonard usually spends an hour or so each day patrolling his grocery store, which stocks around 1,000 items (compared to an average of 15,000 items found in a larger supermarket). His philosophy is simple: He gives the people only what they want—nothing more, nothing less.

People who visit his store never wait in line to check out with their groceries. Leonard makes sure that each of his 29 registers is always open. And he listens to his customers when they tell him something. He treats all customers who walk through his doors as if they were royalty, because in Leonard's eyes, they are.

Here's a story Leonard likes to share about a customer who came into the store during the holiday season. She was trying to return a carton of eggnog that she claimed was

spoiled. Leonard told her that about 300 other customers had bought eggnog from the same batch without a problem. In short, he told her she was wrong, and she wouldn't be getting a refund.

The woman complained that she would never shop there again, and after she left the store Leonard realized what a mistake he had made. In fact, within a few months he erected a monument to his customers and memorialized his own mistake. A three-ton

At Your Service

Successful consultants make it a goal to live by these ten credos:

1. *Accept full responsibility for all your actions.* Concentrate on giving your very best, no matter how good, bad, or indifferent your client may be.

2. *Develop an attitude of optimism and positive expectation.* Begin to expect the very best from yourself, and soon others around you will see what a powerful force you present. Remember, optimists are simply people who have learned how to discipline their attitudes to their advantage.

3. *Motivate yourself to have a "never give up" style.* Make your clients feel that you are there for them no matter what. In other words, you will go above and beyond the call of duty to fulfill your end of the agreement.

4. *Keep improving your communications skills.* When there is a breakdown in communication, chaos results. Practice your listening skills. Sometimes clients may not be clear about what they want; be certain you understand what is expected of you.

5. *Believe in yourself.* When you have a high level of self-esteem, the sky is the limit.

6. *Be flexible.* Any consultant who can maintain a high degree of flexibility will gain a good reputation and have no trouble attracting new clients.

7. *Set goals.* When you have a plan of action with certain goals in mind, your goals will be easier to achieve. Remember, if you fail to plan, you plan to fail.

8. *Organize yourself.* This will impress your clients and help you become a more successful consultant.

9. *Seek more than one solution to a problem.* And always look for creative ways to solve those problems. Walt Disney was a firm believer in the power of brainstorming; you should be, too!

10. *Be happy!* When you're happy, those around you will be happy, too.

granite boulder stands at the entryway to the store, emblazoned with the store's two cardinal rules. "Rule Number 1: The Customer Is Always Right. Rule Number 2: If The Customer Is Ever Wrong, Go Back And Reread Rule Number 1."

Now, when you think about offering the best customer service possible, remember Stew Leonard. In fact, your goal should be to top his customer service philosophy—if that's even possible!

> ## Smart Tip
> **Tip...**
>
> Remember that your customers are the most important aspect of your consulting business; without them, you—and your business—will never survive!

Developing a Win-Win Style

To succeed as a consultant, you need to develop a win-win style of management. This means that both you and your client must view everything that is done as something positive, as a means of moving forward, as a way of solving a problem.

Your ultimate success depends on your ability to use your inner resources and strengths. You hold the secrets to winning; without unlocking those secrets, you are doomed to failure. Do whatever it takes to solve your clients' problems and challenges. By doing so, both you and your client come out winners.

Melinda Patrician, a public relations consultant in Arlington, Virginia, has some advice for people who are trying to make it in the consulting field. "One thing I would highly recommend," she says, "particularly to women who are consulting for organizations, is to get to know what the power structure is in that organization and get to know the support staff as well as your contact person."

As a consultant, you may feel as if you have to be all things to all people. And sometimes in trying to do so, you may be setting yourself up to fail. Let's examine five problem areas you need to consider before accepting any consulting position:

1. *You aren't able to identify the real problem.* You need to look beyond your specialty to determine where a client's solution may be. Bear, Delaware, consultant John Riddle once had a client whose nonprofit organization had grown out of control. The organization was having difficulty meeting its monthly bills, and its contributions from foundations and corporations had been steadily declining over the years. Yet it kept growing and offering its health-related services throughout the state. When Riddle first took the organization on as a client, he thought they simply needed a rock-solid fundraising plan, one that would dramatically increase their ability to attract the contributions they needed to stay open. But after carefully interviewing many of their key employees and managers, he realized that their fundraising plans were OK; they needed a consultant who was skilled in nonprofit reorganization.

2. *You promise more than you can deliver.* While all consultants like to think they can solve everyone's problem on time and under budget, the reality of the business is that you can't. And once you recognize that fact of the consulting life, you won't promise too much. It is very easy to listen to your client talk about the problems in the organization. The hard part comes when you sit down to actually solve the problems. Don't offer solutions that you are not 100 percent sure from the beginning you can carry out.

> **Smart Tip** Tip...
>
> Your attitude is your most priceless possession and can make the difference between success and failure as a consultant. Take time for an attitude check every day; it should always be in a positive mode.

3. *You fail to be specific about the role you will be playing.* Too often a consultant will sign a contract with a client and not have a clear understanding of what the client expects. Make sure you and your client put in writing what tasks you will be performing and how you will accomplish them. (You'll find some tips for creating effective contracts in Chapter 13.)

4. *You fail to treat each client as an individual.* Countless nonprofit organizations spend thousands of dollars on consultant after consultant, and each time the client hopes that the consultant will help the organization. Far too often, consultants come in, listen to a client's problems and concerns, and will already be mentally calculating how many pages the boilerplate report needs to be. Some consultants get very excited because they know they will be able to use a report that they have presented to other organizations they have worked for in the past. All they need to do, really, is to change the names, dates, and figures. "After all," the consultant thinks, "all these problems are the same." But if you want to succeed in the consulting world, you'd better learn to treat all clients, and their problems, individually.

5. *You may not be qualified to get the job done.* Occasionally, you may come across a client who offers you a job you know you would like to have (either for the money or for the prestige of working for that particular client), but you may not be qualified to do. Know when you should take a job and when you should turn down a job. If you are offered a job you would never be able to do on your own, consider bringing in an associate on a temporary basis to help you. (We'll talk more about hiring additional help in Chapter 7.)

As a consultant, it is your job to market yourself and sell your services to those clients who need your help. Make sure both you and your clients are happy with the results.

Setting Up
Shop

Now that you have a pretty good idea of
the background and skills you'll need to be a successful consultant, it's time to start laying the groundwork for establishing
that business. This chapter covers selecting a location for your
business (a home office is usually a great choice for a consultant), writing a business plan, naming your business, and

addressing all those other little details (like getting a business license) that are necessary to get your fledgling enterprise up and running.

Staying Home

Your consulting business will probably not require a large initial capital investment, particularly if you consider operating out of your home. (Certain deed restrictions and local laws may prohibit you from doing this; check with an attorney before you proceed.)

There are many advantages to having a home office.

- *Low overhead expenses.* You don't have to worry about paying rent or utilities for an office; you will greatly appreciate this feature since you haven't yet established a paying regular client base.
- *Flexibility.* There's little doubt that operating as a consultant at home gives you a lot of flexibility. You can set your own hours and take time off as you need it.

Home Court Disadvantages

Of course, running a business from your home isn't all fun and games. There are a few disadvantages to operating out of your home.

○ *Loneliness.* If you're used to working in a large office setting with plenty of people, you may experience culture shock when you first open your consulting business at home. Make sure you develop a network of friends and other associates to talk with on a regular basis.

○ *The temptation to do all those "home" things.* It takes a well-disciplined person to work at home. You must be able to say to yourself, "I am at work. I will not stop and do the laundry, mow the lawn, or shovel snow."

○ *The stigma of owning a rinky-dink homebased business.* Some potential clients may not hire you because you don't have an office downtown. But since the number of homebased businesses has been growing over the past decade and those businesses have been earning the respect they are due, this is becoming less of an issue.

○ *Constant interruptions.* Family members, friends, and neighbors may not respect your working time and space and may feel they can interrupt you any time they want.

○ *Lack of meeting space.* You may be limited when it comes to seeing clients in your home office depending on how large your house is.

- *End of rush-hour nightmares.* For anyone who has had to commute to and from a job during rush hour, a home office is a welcome change of pace. "I've had to do an awful lot of driving in my career, so I love working at home—I wouldn't trade it for the world," says Hockessin, Delaware, public relations consultant Bill Metten.
- *Tax-deductibility.* The IRS has relaxed the rules for people who work at home, but check with your accountant or income tax preparer to see if you qualify for this deduction.

Smart Tip Tip...
Voice mail is an invaluable tool for homebased businesses. Not only does it make you appear more professional to callers, but it ensures that you'll never miss an important call because you're already on the line or you're using a dial-up internet service.

And speaking of your home office, we recommend that, right from day one, you establish a specific place to work that's devoted strictly to business and has actual office furniture. The reasons are simple. Having an office gives you a place to go to everyday where your work is done—not unlike the setup you may have had when you were working for someone else in corporate America. It also serves as a reminder that real work must be done there to support yourself and your family, lessening the allure of outside distractions. Finally, a dedicated space will help you draw the line between your business and home life, which is really important when you're self-employed. Especially in the early days of a new business, it can be very tempting to throw yourself wholeheartedly into the business to the exclusion of your significant other, children, and personal interests. Being able to walk out of the spare bedroom that serves as your office and close the door behind you will help you to have a life—which, if you'll recall, is probably one of the reasons you decided to start your business in the first place.

"The real benefit of having an office in the basement away from the living areas is that it helps me to concentrate on the job," says Merrily Schiavone, a graphic design consultant in Newark, Delaware. "It also keeps me from running upstairs to make a bed!"

Smart Tip Tip...
Check with your local civic association to see if they have any objection to your operating a service business from your home. It's better to make friends with them before you run into any problems.

If you don't have the luxury of having a spare room that can be converted into an office, all is not lost. A corner of the living room partitioned off with a screen (available at any home décor store), a closet converted into a workstation, or even a pantry will do. Just be sure to pick a place that's outside the mainstream of family activity, and make sure it's clear to your spouse and kids that your "special place" is for work only. You'll also want to make sure your family understands your business phone is sacrosanct and may never be answered by anyone other than you.

We'll talk more about what it takes to equip your workspace in Chapter 6. In the meantime, let's talk about what else it takes to make this new business go.

It's a Plan

The last time you went on a two-week vacation by car, did you just pack up the kids, toss a few bathing suits into the trunk, and hit the road? Probably not. As you know, it takes careful planning to get to any destination—and that goes double for when you're starting your own business.

As a result, one of the very first tasks you should undertake during the start-up phase of your consultancy should be the crafting of a carefully constructed business plan. Besides outlining your plans, goals, and strategies, a business plan can be helpful if you ever have to approach a lending institution for funds.

You don't have to be a writer to draw up a viable plan—you just need vision and, hopefully, a little analytical skill to help you size up your market and your competition, then create a document that addresses the opportunities. But if you do need assistance, it's readily available from sources like your local Small Business Development Center (found in the Federal section of the Yellow Pages under the SBA or by logging on to www.sba.gov/sbdc). You should also check out your local bookstore or library for books or software packages that can make the writing process much easier.

Making it Legal

This is another one of those decisions you should make early in the business planning process. Basically, there are four types of legal structures: sole proprietorship, partnership, corporation, and limited liability company (LLC).

The legal form you choose will very much depend on your personal situation and how much risk you're willing to take. Many consultants, like Huntington Beach, California, public relations consultant Susan Bock, chose to start as a sole proprietor because it's the easiest type of business to form.

"I originally thought I'd work as a sole proprietorship until I had a sense of where I wanted the business to go," Bock says. "My financial planner and attorney also suggested I wait to make a choice. Eventually, I decided this was the best choice for me."

The best choice for Schiavone was an S Corporation because of its many benefits. "Overall it's just easier for me when it comes to taxes and other matters," she says.

David McMullen, a computer consultant in Costa Mesa, California, is about to form an LLC after operating as a sole proprietor for the first two years. "Every quarter I've had revenue growth, and I'm now clearing quite a bit more than when I started," he says. "Back then, I didn't feel like forking out the money to become 'legal,' but since I don't want anyone coming after my personal assets, it's time to change my legal status."

With all the variables involved in selecting the most appropriate form of business for your consultancy, you'll find it helpful to talk to an attorney. Chapter 5 will discuss how to pick an attorney who will meet your needs.

The Name of the Game

What's in a name? Plenty, especially if you want your business to be successful. When selecting a name for your consulting business (also known as a trade name), choose carefully. Take a few moments and browse through the local Yellow Pages; this exercise will often give you a few good lessons on what not to name your business. Look under "Consultants," and you will see a wide variety of consulting names, everything from ABC Consulting (do they teach you the alphabet?), to Kite Associates (do they teach you to make kites, or just fly them?), to The Dolphin Consulting Group (fill in your favorite "Flipper" joke). Creativity is fine, but unless your goal is to provide a good laugh or confuse potential clients, then take some time choosing a name before hanging out your shingle for all the world to see.

Merrily Schiavone came up with the name AdHelp for her consulting business, which reflects the services she provided. "I'm actually helping people with their advertising, so I just put the words 'ad' and 'help' together," says Schiavone. "And I knew that because the name began with the letter 'a,' it would always be listed near the top."

Riddle chose Blue Moon Communications as the name of his consulting business because he thought it was catchy and didn't limit the services he might provide in the future. It also adds a little whimsy and appealed to his sense of fun.

Other entrepreneurs have found the monikers for their businesses right in front of their noses—they used variations of their names and counted on their recognition within the community.

As a consultant, you want to portray an aura of professionalism, so try to stay away from cutesy names for your company. If you aren't sure what to call your business, try something simple like "John Doe and Associates" or even "John Doe, Consultant." Just be sure that when

Tip...

Smart Tip

When deciding on a name for your consulting business, be sensitive to how that name might translate into another language. For example, if you will be dealing with non-native-speaking clients (even in this country), you want to make sure your business name is not offensive when translated into their native language.

you advertise in the telephone book, you are specific about the type of consulting services you offer. (For example, if you offer management consulting services, make sure you are placed in that category.)

Paper Trail

Once you've selected your business name, your next step should be to register it with your local government—usually the county. Most states require you to file paperwork to establish your business name as unique, even if you're using your own name as part of the company name. Known as a "dba," which is short for "doing business as," an assumed name establishes that you are the only one permitted to operate under that name in the jurisdiction. An assumed name is also necessary so you can accept and cash checks in your company name, as well as set up a business checking account (which is always recommended).

The fee for a dba is quite nominal (around $30 to $60). As part of the registration process, the county will do a search of local businesses to ascertain that your name is

---

Information, Please

The internet can be a consultant's best friend. Once you become internet-savvy, you'll discover the plethora of information in cyberspace that will help you as you grow and expand your consulting practice. Check out these web sites:

○ *Association of Professional Consultants (www.consultapc.org).* This is an excellent resource for consultants in all fields. Members have access to publicity and promotions, professional workshops and courses, and a whole array of business information of interest to consulting professionals.

○ *Expert Marketplace (www.expert-market.com).* This unique website contains listings of more than 20,000 consulting firms and individuals. With its searchable database, you will have no trouble finding consultants you can network with in locations around the country.

○ *The SBA (www.sba.gov).* The SBA is an excellent online resource for consultants who are just starting out in their own practices. Everything from advice on promoting your business to financial planning is available with the click of your mouse.

Beware!
It's tempting to try to take on all the work that comes your way when you first start out, but don't do it, or you'll burn out fast.

unique. In case the name you have chosen has already been taken (which is not uncommon), be sure to have a couple of extra names in reserve.

While you're checking into that dba, you should inquire about any licenses needed to operate legally in your community. In most cases, this is a mere formality—most communities are small business friendly and won't have any objections to your fledgling operation. The exception might be if your business will generate a lot of traffic that could be disruptive to your neighborhood, including having employees who are not related to you working in your home and parking vehicles on the street. In that case, you may have to apply for a zoning variance, which is issued by your local government. Variances are not automatically granted, so if you really intend to entertain a lot of clients or hold frequent business meetings, it might be a better idea to rent some office space on an as-needed basis.

A business license is also usually quite inexpensive—perhaps $10 or $20—and is renewable annually. Save yourself some time in line at the county courthouse by checking to see if you can apply for the license online.

It's possible you'll need other state or even federal licenses to operate, depending upon the kind of work you do. Check with your state licensing department for additional information.

You may find the paperwork requirements to be minimal. Jeffery Bartlett, a marketing research consultant in Harrisburg, Pennsylvania, says there is no special license needed for the work his firm performs. "We provide focus group facilities to our clients," he says, "and we only need a business license to operate."

In addition to a business license, if you're a consultant in a specialized field, such as accounting, you will probably need a professional license to do business. Check with the appropriate state agency for additional information.

Calling in the
Professionals

Now that you're on your way to establishing your consultancy, it's time to think about the experts you'll need to keep your business running. At the minimum, you'll need a trio of professionals on your team: an attorney, an accountant, and an insurance agent. While it can be hard to part with the cash for professional fees this early in the game, it's a critical move. Hiring skilled professionals will allow you to hand over work that you're probably not an expert at doing anyway while freeing you to devote all your time to the work you do best.

Having these pros on your management team is beneficial in yet another way. Professional advisors make your business look much more stable, solid, and professional when it comes time to approach a banker for financial assistance.

Legal Eagles

Most people think of attorneys as someone they hire to get them out of a jam. But as American banker and financier J.P. Morgan said, "I don't want a lawyer to tell me what I cannot do. I hire him to tell me how to do what I want to do." For an aspiring entrepreneur, that means having a competent ally to read the fine print of those incomprehensible contracts that no one else reads and steer you around any potential pitfalls caused by legalese. He or she also will be invaluable when you're drafting contracts of your own, if you have a contract dispute, when you're negotiating a business loan, or when you're signing a lease for a lot of money (such as when you decide to move out of your home office). An attorney also can help you with tax issues and the process of selecting a business structure.

Unfortunately, a lot of start-up entrepreneurs shy away from hiring the attorney they need because they think they can't afford one. This is not necessarily the case. While it's true that the services of an attorney in a large firm might be beyond the means of a start-up consultant, it is possible to find someone who can work within your financial boundaries. An attorney in a small one- or two-person practice is usually a good bet, as is someone who charges a flat fee for routine work (like writing letters or setting up a corporation), or one who offers a business start-up package. A start-up package runs about $900 and usually includes the initial consultation and all activities related to the incorporation or LLC process, including the filing of paperwork with your state and other corporate formalities. Alternatively, it's possible to hire an attorney on retainer, which is paid upfront and is drawn against by the attorney as work is completed.

Attorneys typically charge around $100 an hour, although this varies widely depending on

Dollar Stretcher

Because you're not likely to have many legal fees once you've incorporated or consulted with an attorney about your legal business structure, you may find it more cost effective to purchase a prepaid legal plan. After paying a small annual fee, you'll have access to a qualified attorney for services like telephone consultations, letter writing, and contract review. You can find leads to such plans in the Yellow Pages under "Legal Service Plans."

> **Tip...**
>
> **Smart Tip**
>
> To keep your financial management fees under control, ask your accountant to help you set up basic ledgers and record-keeping systems for logging data and tracking receivables. If you're computer savvy, you can easily do this yourself using a software program like QuickBooks Pro.

where you are doing business. Fortunately, there are simple ways to keep down the cost of legal fees. First, keep calls to your attorney to a minimum, since he or she is on the clock every time you call. For the same reason, be sure to have all the information and documents you need right at hand when you do call or meet. You can also ask your attorney to estimate the amount of time he or she thinks a project will take so there are no surprises later, and you should ask for an itemized statement of services to make sure you're receiving the services for which you're being billed.

While you'll find a lot of attorneys listed in the phone book, it's usually wiser to ask business colleagues or other small-business owners for a recommendation. Your local chamber of commerce or other business organizations may also be good sources of leads, as are attorney referral services, which can be found in most major metropolitan areas.

Bookmakers

Even if you have always done your own taxes and can balance your checkbook with ease, you still will need the services of a professional accountant for your business. Keeping the books can be very labor intensive and siphons off crucial time you'll need to manage your consultancy. You'll also find it's a great relief to be able to count on someone experienced to keep your balance sheet balanced, make sure estimated tax payments are made promptly, and so on. This is not to say, however, that you can't do the basic bookkeeping yourself using a spreadsheet program like Microsoft Excel or QuickBooks Pro. But you'll want to engage the services of an accountant for the complicated tasks, including creating profit and loss statements, making financial projections and forecasting cash flow, setting up accounting systems, and interpreting tax law.

> **Tip...**
>
> **Smart Tip**
>
> Remember to keep the receipt for every item purchased for the business. Besides needing good insurance records in case of a business loss, you'll need this information at tax time since everything from office supplies to computer equipment can be added up for a tax deduction on Form 1040, Schedule C.

As with attorneys, accountants' hourly rates vary widely depending on factors such as type of practice, location, expertise, and education. In New Hampshire, for instance, the average

It's Technical

There's one more expert you should consider adding to your stable of business professionals: a savvy and experienced computer consultant. Unless you're a computer consultant yourself, chances are your knowledge of what makes computers go is pretty limited. That means when something goes wrong, you may not have the foggiest idea how to fix it and you could waste valuable time trying. A computer expert can help you avoid that kind of aggravation.

To find a knowledgeable consultant, ask around among your friends and business associates (or even the local computer superstore). You'll want to find someone who makes house calls (which costs more but is worth it because you won't have to unhook your cables) and can explain in plain English what's wrong and how it can be fixed. And by the way, even if you are a computer consultant, having one on call isn't a bad idea—after all, that frees you up to consult and make money.

hourly wage of an accountant with a bachelor's degree is just over $21, according to the New Hampshire Job Outlook and Locator, a state publication that lists occupations by industry; while a survey by PCPS Management for the Virginia Society of CPAs says that a certified public accountant in a small accounting firm would have a billing rate of $83 an hour.

For a referral to a reputable accountant, speak to your attorney, banker, or other local small-business owners, or contact the American Institute of Certified Public Accountants' branch in your state. You also can find a professional accountant on the www.accountant-finder.com web site. When choosing an accountant, try to select someone with small-business experience since he or she is more likely to understand your concerns and finances. You'll find additional bookkeeping strategies and techniques in Chapter 12.

Going for Broker

One of the more surprising things you'll discover about this business of owning your own business is the amount of insurance you should have to protect your assets and your livelihood. That's why you need to establish a relationship with a capable insurance broker. A broker is usually preferable to an agent because a broker represents many different insurance products from many different companies, but an insurance agent is employed by a single company and sells only that company's products. As a result, you may find that a broker can get you better policies and rates.

You can find dozens of insurance broker/agent listings in the Yellow Pages, but as with the other professionals discussed here, it's usually best to ask a business acquaintance or attorney for a referral. To find someone with that all-important small-business acumen, ask to see a client list when you're shopping around for a broker.

Once you've selected your broker, you'll want to work closely with him or her to determine exactly how much coverage you will need. Basically, the dollar amount of coverage you'll buy will depend on the amount of risk you're willing to take; i.e., the more coverage you have, the less likely you are to be stuck making an out-of-pocket payment in the event of a business catastrophe or error.

Getting Covered

Although there is insurance available to cover just about any contingency that might occur while you are self-employed (and your agent will be more than happy to sell it to you), small-business owners like consultants generally can't afford to insure against everything that might go wrong. Nor would you want to. It's better to purchase just enough coverage to save your company from ruin in the event of a disaster (both manmade and divinely wrought). And tempting though it may be, don't skimp on important coverage. It's not worth the risk of losing everything you've built to save a few bucks.

Among the types of personal insurance consultants commonly carry are:

- *Health*. Now that you're self-employed, you'll have to shoulder this cost on your own. Fortunately, health insurance premiums are now 100 percent deductible for self-employed persons—and their employees—when they report a net profit on Schedule C, C-EZ, or F. See IRS Publication 535, *Business Expenses*, for more information.

- *Disability*. If you can't work due to injury or illness, this insurance will replace a percentage of your gross income. Having this type of policy can mean the difference between staying solvent and going bankrupt when you're self-employed, yet new business owners tend to forego purchasing disability insurance in the interest of saving money. Don't make that potentially devastating error.

- *Life*. This type of insurance is important for two reasons: It protects your family or significant other in case of your death, and it may be required before you can obtain a loan from a bank or other financial institution.

The types of business insurance you may need are:

- *General business liability*. This is a must because it protects you (and your employees, if applicable) if you're sued when someone is hurt or accidental damage is caused on or to a client's property.

- *Equipment.* This type of policy covers damage to or loss of equipment due to fire or theft. It's a good idea for entrepreneurs who work out of their homes, especially since homeowners insurance usually doesn't cover business equipment. Instead, a separate policy or possibly a rider is needed.

- *Property.* If you're operating out of a commercial space, you'll need property insurance to protect both the building you're working out of (if you own it) and its contents. If you're working at home, you don't need this.

- *Business interruption.* This type of policy pays the cost of your normal business expenses if you're unable to operate due to a natural disaster (like a hurricane), a fire, theft, or other insured loss. It may also pay for equipment losses.

- *Errors and omissions.* Imagine how you'd feel if mistakes in the work you did for a client caused him or her financial losses. Then imagine how much worse you'd feel if the client sued you. That's why you might want to consider buying this type of liability insurance.

- *Workers' compensation.* This nonnegotiable insurance is required by all 50 states and covers your employees in the event of injury or illness on the job (but not you—as the owner you don't count as an employee). The amount of coverage necessary and the percentage of salary paid to employees under workers' comp vary by state.

Because managing risk can be a complex issue and because you don't want to buy less insurance than you need, it really is a good idea to find a reputable insurance broker to help you make some decisions. In the meantime, we've included an insurance planning worksheet that you can use to compare policies and premiums if you'd like to do some of the work on your own.

Business Insurance Planning Worksheet

Type	Required	Premium	Payment Schedule
Health			
Disability			
Life			
General business liability			
Equipment			
Property (casualty)			
Business interruption			
Errors and omissions			
Workers' compensation			
Other			
Other			
Total annual cost:			$

Tools of
the Trade

Running an office out of your home can save you a lot of money because you won't be saddled right out of the box with high overhead costs such as rent and utilities. Instead, what you'll spend your start-up dollars on will be the basic tools you need to run a successful business. Those tools, which include office furniture, equipment, and supplies, are discussed in this chapter.

To estimate how much cash you'll need to get your business up and running, use the blank start-up chart you'll find on page 50. This work sheet lists the typical types of expenses you can expect to incur and has spaces where you can pencil in other projected expenses as you research your start-up costs. As you do this exercise, you may find it helpful to refer to the sample start-up expenses worksheet on page 49, which lists the expenses for two hypothetical consulting businesses: Retail Management Consulting, a sole proprietorship and low-end startup; and David Jones and Associates, a high-end startup that operates as an S corporation and has one full-time employee (the owner) and one administrative assistant.

Beware!

Home office expenses (like the percentage of your mortgage payment, utility bills, etc., that pertain to the business) are deductible only if you are organized as a sole proprietorship or S corporation. To take the deduction, you'll have to file Form 8829, *Expenses for Business Use of Your Home*, and Schedule C with your taxes.

Now here's a rundown of what you may need to start your business on the right foot.

Office Furniture and Equipment

In Chapter 4, we tried to dissuade you from setting up shop on your dining room table or the ironing board in the laundry room. The reason is simple: No one can work effectively that way. Rather, you need a comfortable, user-friendly space where you can park yourself, possibly for hours on end, and where you'll have easy access to a computer, office supplies, and the other tools of your trade. Ideally, you should set up a basic office consisting of a desk or computer workstation, an ergonomic office chair, a sturdy two- or four-drawer file cabinet with drawers that extend fully, and perhaps a bookcase or two. Unless you expect to entertain clients in your home office, there's no reason why you can't keep your furniture costs down by purchasing inexpensive ready-to-assemble or secondhand furniture in good condition. Thrift shops are an excellent source of gently used furniture, as are newspaper classifieds and auction marketplaces like eBay. If you prefer new furniture, visit an office supply store such as Office Depot or Staples. They carry a wide selection of reasonably priced desks that run $50 to $250 and chairs that cost $50 to $200.

Personal Computer and Software

Since most consulting jobs require you to churn out consulting proposals, contracts, reports, invoices, and other documents, a reliable personal computer is a must. (News flash for anyone using an older and slower computer: This means you, too!) Fortunately, you don't have to spend a lot of money to get a really great computer. For instance, at press time Dell was offering the Dimension 3000 computer system with a

40GB hard drive, 17-inch monitor, CD or DVD drive, and WordPerfect software for just $549. Add on useful extras like a laser or inkjet printer, flat-screen monitor (which is easier on the eyes), and various supplies, and a complete system may run closer to $1,500.

To run the common business software packages efficiently, your system should have a speed of 2.40GHz, with at least 80GB memory and 512MB SDRAM. It should come equipped with a CD-ROM drive so you can load most software packages and download data to CDs, as well as internal fax and modem cards, both of which are standard on all but the very lowest priced computers. Other useful optional equipment that's especially necessary for a writer, public relations consultant, or graphic arts designer includes a scanner ($100 to $300, depending on the resolution) and a portable USB flash drive for storing and transporting data. Also, if you deal with art or the written word, you should consider purchasing the largest monitor you can afford, since it can help prevent eyestrain. A 19-inch monitor starts at about $600, although prices are dropping fast. It's not uncommon to see these monitors on sale for half that amount at the electronic superstores.

> **Tip...**
>
> **Smart Tip**
> Depending on how much time you spend on the road, you may find it useful to have a notebook computer to carry along with you. They're lightweight (usually no more than a few pounds), but they can handle everything your desktop does. They're also quite affordable at around $1,000.

The most commonly used office productivity packages are Microsoft Office and QuickBooks Pro. Microsoft Office Professional includes Word, Excel, PowerPoint (a must for presentation materials), Access (for database management), and Outlook e-mail. It currently retails for $499. QuickBooks is an easy-to-use accounting package that keeps your financial records straight, manages your business checking account, and prints checks. The current edition, QuickBooks Basic, retails for $199.95, and the upgrade is just $99.95.

Fax Machines

With the overabundance of junk faxes that waste your paper and ink and the fax cards that are standard equipment in most computers, full-size fax machines are becoming less common. But they still may come in handy to receive those important incoming messages if you don't want to leave your computer on 24/7. The good news is that fax machines are really quite inexpensive these days—a multifunction machine that also scans, copies, and prints can be had for as low as $200. Be sure to check around before you buy; discount electronics stores like Circuit City often sell these inkjet fax machines for the best prices.

Home office users often install their fax machines on their regular business phone line, but if you think you'll use your fax a lot you may want to put it on a dedicated telephone line. It's about $40 to $60 to install a separate line.

Phones

Telephones come in all sizes and price ranges, but avoid the impulse to cut corners on your business phone equipment. Rather, buy the best model you can afford—after all, you're likely to be on the phone a lot. A standard two-line speakerphone with auto-redial, memory dial, flashing lights, mute button, and other useful features will run $40 to $150, while a top-of-the-line model can cost $250 or more. One good source for high-quality telecommunications equipment is Hello Direct (see Appendix), which carries a line of professional business telephones.

Smart Tip

If your cellular phone is used strictly for business, it's 100 percent deductible on your business taxes.

With voice mail, it's a wonder anyone uses an answering machine anymore. But this old stand-by technology does have its good points, including the fact that you can tell at a glance whether you have a message waiting. A stand-alone digital answering machine costs $15 to $200; a cordless phone/answering machine combo will run from $50 to $200.

A cellular phone is an absolute must for a consultant, especially if your job entails rolling out programs that require frequent updates or if you manage on-site projects.

Hire Office

If you can't work out of your home, but you also can't afford to lease traditional office space at the genesis of your business, consider an office-sharing arrangement instead. For a monthly fee, you can rent a fully furnished private space (usually 500 square feet or less) in the office building in the neighborhood of your choice. Such rentals often come with everything you need to make a good impression on a prospect or client, including a reception area with a receptionist, a telephone answering service, a conference room, and a genuine business address for mail and package deliveries. For an extra fee, you may be able to obtain administrative support, photocopying, videoconferencing, and other useful business services.

If you don't need space on an ongoing basis, you may be able to rent space on a per-use basis from an office-sharing company. Under this arrangement, you rent an office space for just a few hours or a day here and there on a first-come, first-served basis.

You can find office-sharing companies in the Yellow Pages under "Office & Desk Space Rental Service."

Today's wireless plans are very cost-effective and include hundreds of minutes of calling time, text messaging, and other useful features. Picture phones are also very handy for sending photos of job sites, products, and other details to your clients.

Since your usage level will probably be high, look for a plan that includes a large number of monthly minutes and free weekend calling. For example, one deal offered by a big-name cellular provider includes 400 minutes of calling time and unlimited nights and weekends for $39.99. For $79.99, the same cellular provider offers unlimited nationwide calling and Broadband access to the internet. The cell phone itself can run up to $240 for the latest models or under $100 for a basic model. Some cellular companies (like T-Mobile) still offer a free phone with service activation. See "Services" on page 47 for a more complete rundown of monthly service charges.

If that isn't enough technology for you, you can add a pager to your telecommunications arsenal. With the proliferation of cellular phones, you may find your clients would rather dial you up directly than wait for a call back, but pagers are small and inexpensive. A new alphanumeric pager costs as little as $20 or may be free when you activate service with some providers.

Toll-Free Numbers

Twenty years ago, only large corporations were able to afford toll-free telephone numbers. But advances in technology have made it possible for nearly every business to have a toll-free number, no matter what its size.

John Riddle, the Bear, Delaware, fundraising and editorial consultant, believes that depending on who your target market is, a toll-free number can be the deciding factor in whether your consulting business succeeds. He certainly has used a toll-free number to great advantage. When he was selling ad space in his fundraising newsletters, he discovered that his toll-free number was his secret weapon.

"Many times I asked advertisers why they selected my newsletter to advertise in, and more often than not, their reply was, 'Because you had a toll-free telephone number,'" Riddle says. "It was my only advantage over the competition."

If you are considering a toll-free telephone number, contact more than one company and get bids. Don't forget to compare the services you will be receiving, too.

Copy Machines

While not an absolute necessity, a copy machine can be a very convenient addition to your home office. A basic portable desktop model costs as little as $100, but a digital model that kicks out up to 20 copies per minute at 600 dpi, sends faxes, and scans documents at 400 dpi runs about $4,000. Remarkably, the footprint of these workhorses is quite small—often less than 30 square inches—which makes them perfect for home office use. Keep in mind, however, that if you need to do a big copying job, especially one that requires collated, stapled, double-sided copies, your best bet is to take it somewhere such as Kinko's. Your time is better spent consulting than copying.

Supplies you'll need for your copier include copy paper and toner cartridges, both of which are readily available from your local office supply store. A case of copy paper (ten reams) will run about $25, and a toner cartridge for a personal copier (which yields about 2,000 copies) is around $100. A digital copier toner cartridge (such as for the Canon imageCLASS 2300N) sells for about $200 and makes about 10,000 copies.

Postage

If you expect to do large or frequent mailings either for yourself or your clients, you really should consider investing in a postage meter. You'll pay at least $20 a month to lease a standard postage meter, and then you'll pay for postage as you go, either online at www.usps.com or at the post office. (For bulk mailings, you'll also need a permit for which you'll pay a $150 annual fee.) Alternatively, you can rent a small-business postage meter and scale kit like the one sold by Pitney Bowes. The cost to rent this type of equipment starts at $20 monthly; you must also ante up for the cost of postage and supplies such as ink and mailing labels. Incidentally, it's not possible to buy a postage machine outright. Only the USPS and authorized meter manufacturers can own them, but they'll be happy to rent you one as long as you keep those lease payments coming.

You also should have a postage scale to make sure you're affixing enough postage to your outgoing mail. A manual scale costs $10 to $25; a digital scale runs $40 to $200. If you send more than 20 items a day or use priority or expedited mailing services on a regular basis, you should consider purchasing a programmable electronic scale, which will run $70 to $250.

Office Supplies

You probably can launch your business using whatever pens, paper, Post-its and other office supplies you already have on hand around the house. To fill out your start-up supplies, budget about $30. And here's a time-saving tip: The larger office supply chain stores usually will deliver your order of $50 or more directly to your doorstep in about 24 hours and at no extra charge.

You'll also need a supply of business cards, letterhead and envelopes, and brochures. A quick print shop like American Speedy Printing or an online printing company like ColorPrintingCentral.com can design and produce these items for you. (We've listed a few companies in the Appendix that you can check out.) To get the most competitive quote, try using an online source like Print Quote USA (www.printquoteusa.com). All you do is type in the specs for your job and the web site will do the rest. A casual price survey revealed that 1,000 full-color 8½-by-11-inch brochures printed on good-quality paper costs around $350. Business cards start at around $25 for 1,000 one-color business cards from an office supply superstore like Office Depot, and a box of 500 sheets of one-color letterhead on linen or laid stock is just $75.

Services

Now that you've estimated the cost of all the equipment you're likely to need, here's what it should cost to make it all operate:

- *Phone and fax.* These expenses will run you approximately $33 per line per month, as well as about $12 to $18 extra for voice mail. You'll probably also want to have call waiting, call forwarding, and caller ID, so it pays to check with your regional phone company to find out what types of money-saving packages they offer. These bundled packages often include long-distance minutes as well, which makes them a great value.

- *Cellular.* Typical packages that include voice mail and other standard features run anywhere from $29.95 to $79.95 per month and include 400 or more minutes of peak calling time. You're usually committed to a multiyear contract when you sign up, although you may be able to pay an activation fee of around $30 instead if you don't want to commit.

- *Pagers.* These are a great value at $72 or less for a full year of service that's billed upfront, either annually or quarterly.

- *Toll-free numbers.* The costs can vary widely (and wildly), so you should contact your local phone service provider for a quote. For example, AT&T, the grand-daddy of the telecommunications industry, charges a $35 monthly usage fee for standard billing plans plus a $15-per-month service charge for each toll-free routing arrangement as well as up to 6.9 cents per minute. On the other hand, Carolinanet (http:carolinanetnuvio.com) —which offers local area code service in 46 states—charges a one-time activation fee of $9.99 plus $4.99 a month, which includes 100 incoming minutes per month.

- *Internet.* There is a dizzying array of options when it comes to internet service. Basically, there are five different ways to connect. A dial-up connection through an ISP is the least expensive at $20 to $25 per month, but it's also the slowest of the options. An ISDN line connects and transmits faster. You'll pay about $50 a

> **Fun Fact**
> Want to check to see whether you can secure a memorable phone number for your business, like 1-888-CONSULT? (Sorry, that one's not available.) Then go to AT&T's web site at http://businessesales.att.com/products_services/tollfree product_catalogdisplay.jhtml, where you can plug in the toll-free number of your choice and find out if it's been taken.

Smart Tip

Tip...

If you prefer to keep your personal mail separate from your business mail, a post office box or a box at a mailing center like Mail Boxes Etc. is a great idea. The rental fee is about $10 to $20 a month.

month for the ISDN line itself, plus an additional $20 to $25 a month for an ISP. A DSL line is even faster and will cost about $30 to $40 per month for basic service. Cable modem service, offered through your local cable TV company, is lightning fast and fairly reasonable at about $40 a month on top of your regular cable TV bill. Finally, if you're a satellite rather than cable TV subscriber, you may be able to get Broadband high-speed satellite internet service. A typical plan costs $600 for the necessary equipment, $50 for setup, and $99 a month for residential service.

Vehicle

Even if your consulting practice keeps you in your home office most of the time, eventually you'll have to hit the road to meet with prospects, oversee projects or events, or schmooze with clients over lunch. For this reason, an attractive vehicle in good repair is a must. The good news is you can depreciate the cost of your vehicle on your income taxes. The bad news is only the percentage of the vehicle that's actually used for business can be depreciated. So if you're also using your car or other vehicle for family transportation, you'll have to keep careful written mileage records. Additionally, those business miles are also deductible at a cost of 40.5 cents per mile, so that mileage log is really important. For guidance on depreciation, check out IRS Publication 946, *How to Depreciate Property*, and Publication 463, *Travel, Entertainment, Gift, & Auto Expenses*, which can be downloaded from the IRS' web site at www.irs.gov.

While you don't have to drive a dark-colored conservative sedan to make a good impression, keep in mind that many family vehicles (like the family minivan with Cheerios strewn around the back seat, or a mud-splashed pickup) may not send the message that you're a serious consultant who can be trusted with your clients' important work. If you can't afford to buy or lease a new vehicle, at least keep the one you own clean at all times.

The Bottom Line

If you've been entering your estimated costs on the start-up worksheet on page 50, you'll have a pretty accurate idea of how much capital it will take to launch your new consulting business. It's quite likely the costs will be modest, and you'll be able to finance that start-up with personal savings, the way both Huntington Beach, California, consultant Susan Bock and Newark, Delaware, consultant Merrily Schiavone did. But if you think you're going to need a little financial help, it's not too soon to start the financing crusade. See Chapter 12 for tips on obtaining financing.

Sample Equipment and Supplies Start-Up Costs

	Retail Management Consulting	David Jones and Associates
Office Equipment		
Computer, printer	$550	$1,500
Microsoft Office	500	500
Intuit QuickBooks		200
Surge protector	20	20
Multipurpose fax/scanner/copier		300
Copy machine		150
Postage scale	25	150
Phone	70	150
Cell phone	100	100
Answering machine	40	70
Office Furniture		
Desk	200	300
Chair	60	200
File cabinet(s)	100	200
Bookcase(s)	100	200
Office Supplies		
Business cards	25	25
Brochures	350	350
Letterhead, envelopes	125	125
Miscellaneous supplies (pens, folders, etc.)	30	50
Computer/copier paper	25	25
Extra printer cartridges	50	50
Extra fax cartridges		55
Extra copier toner		100
CD-RW disks	25	25
Mouse pad	10	10
Total	**$2,405**	**$4,855**

Equipment and Supplies Start-Up Costs Worksheet

Office Equipment

Computer, printer	$ _____
Microsoft Office	$ _____
Intuit QuickBooks	$ _____
Surge protector	$ _____
Multipurpose fax/scanner/copier	$ _____
Copy machine	$ _____
Postage scale	$ _____
Phone	$ _____
Cell phone	$ _____
Answering machine	$ _____

Office Furniture

Desk	$ _____
Chair	$ _____
File cabinet(s)	$ _____
Bookcase(s)	$ _____

Office Supplies

Business cards	$ _____
Brochures	$ _____
Letterhead, envelopes	$ _____
Miscellaneous supplies (pens, folders, etc.)	$ _____
Computer/copier paper	$ _____
Extra printer cartridges	$ _____
Extra fax cartridges	$ _____
Extra copier toner	$ _____
CD-RW disks	$ _____
Mouse pad	$ _____
Total	**$ _____**

7

Help
Wanted

When you first open the doors to your consulting practice, you may be able to handle all the operations by yourself. But as your business begins to grow, you may need help handling administrative details or completing the actual consulting assignments. You need to make some important decisions. For example, do you really have the time to make

▲

mailing labels and insert your brochure into 1,000 envelopes? Can you afford to spend time doing administrative tasks when you could be using that time more effectively marketing your services—and signing up new clients? To figure out what some of your hiring options are, read on.

A Helping Hand

When the time comes to hire some help, you have several options. One way is to use a secretarial service. A quick look through the Yellow Pages will reveal a number of small secretarial support firms. The rates depend on a variety of factors, including how large or small the organization is and what types of services it provides. Although it pays to shop around, don't select a secretarial service just because it happens to have the lowest prices in town. Instead, ask for references, preferably from other consultants who have used their services, or from small-business owners. A good, reliable support service is worth the price in the long run.

There may come a time, however, when you will find it more cost effective to hire someone to work with you in the office. Hiring a good administrative support person can sometimes mean the difference between success and failure—between obtaining more clients and constantly losing clients.

There are some benefits to having someone in the office with you.

- *You save time and money.* By having someone concentrate on the more routine tasks (opening the mail, filing, answering phones, etc.), you can focus all your

---

Taking a Temp

There are several advantages to hiring temporary employees to help out when you're in a crunch.

- ○ You can have temporary workers for as long as you want them. They are always available to work by the day, week, or month; however often you need them, they will be there.
- ○ You can avoid the headaches involved in the hiring process. Just pick up the telephone, call a local temporary employment agency, and they will take care of everything for you.
- ○ You don't have to worry about employee-related expenses such as taxes, Social Security, and workers' compensation. The temporary agency pays them.
- ○ You pay only for the hours they work. There are no headaches or hassles about downtime or paying for vacations.

---

efforts on recruiting new clients. Think about this: Would you want to lose a $500-per-day client because you were too cheap to hire someone to stuff your brochures into envelopes?

Smart Tip

Check with your local library and bookstore for publications that show you how to write the perfect job description. A few minutes of effort now will help you avoid problems down the road.

- *You don't need to worry about being out of the office.* If you are a one-person operation, it's hard to be on the road marketing your services if you're worried about clients calling and getting your voice mail or answering machine.

- *You have someone to offer another perspective.* Sometimes it can be pretty lonely trying to do everything yourself. Having someone around the office during the day who can offer another perspective can be worthwhile.

But before hanging out that "Help Wanted" sign, first consider using a temporary employee. This can be pricey, but it is sometimes the best solution, especially if your consulting business is seasonal. By hiring a temp, you don't have to worry about laying someone off when business slows down.

Another type of employee who should be mentioned here is the independent contractor (aka freelancer or—yes!—consultant). This is a person who is not on your payroll but represents you and handles your work as though it's his or her own. In exchange, you pay the freelancer either an hourly wage or a salary. You are not obligated to offer benefits, nor do you pay employment taxes, withhold FICA and other taxes, or pony up for workers' compensation insurance.

Although this may sound like a pretty good deal, employing independent contractors can create a minefield of potential problems. The IRS has very strict definitions about the difference between an employee and an independent contractor. To find out what the IRS has to say about this, visit www.irs.gov and type "independent consultants vs. employees" in the search window. If you're seriously interested in using freelancers, you should pick up a copy of Publication 15-A, *Employer's Supplemental Tax Guide*, from your nearest IRS field office. You can also download it from the www.irs.gov web site.

The Hiring Process

When your consulting business becomes so busy that you need to hire someone on a permanent basis, you want to look for the perfect employee. It doesn't matter if you are hiring a secretary, an administrative person, a bookkeeper, or even an associate who will help you with the consulting work. You want an employee who shows up for work early, stays late, and doesn't worry about overtime or comp time, right?

But before you get too excited, realize there's no such thing as a perfect employee. And that's OK, because a perfect person would probably drive you nuts anyway. A good employee is within reach, however, if you first think about what you want that person to do. Be sure to develop an accurate job description that covers all the duties you want the employee to handle.

When creating your job description, take the following into consideration:

- *Decide how many hours a week your new employee will work.* You may find that at least in the beginning of your venture into employee management, a part-time employee (20 to 30 hours a week) will be sufficient. If you're really busy, you may need a full-timer (35 to 40 hours a week) right out of the box.
- *Select a job title.* Titles may not seem important to you, but to some employees, a title is worth more than the money they are getting paid. For example, you might consider changing "Administrative Assistant" to "Administrative Associate." It doesn't matter that the pay and the duties are the same; the title gives the employee a feeling of importance and ownership.
- *Outline the specific responsibilities the employee will handle.* If you don't include everything upfront, you may run into trouble down the road.
- *Define the educational experience required.*
- *Define the additional work-related experience required.*
- *Establish who the employee will report to.*
- *List special physical requirements, if any.* For example, if your office regularly receives boxes of books that weigh more than 40 pounds each, indicate that the employee will have to be physically able to lift them.

Screening Applicants

When you make the decision to hire employees, don't look for potential candidates from among your friends or relatives. If you hire them and they don't work out for whatever reason, you not only lose an employee, you also lose a friend.

Once you place an ad or let friends and business associates know you have an opening, the resumes will start making their way into your life. Although an impressive resume may lead you to believe that a candidate is definitely the one you want to hire, be cautious. It is easy for job applicants to make themselves look better than they really are through well-crafted resumes. This is not to say that most people lie on their resumes (although there has been an increase in resume-related fraud over the past decade), but as the employer, you need to take any claims made on paper with a hefty grain of

Smart Tip

Hiring another consultant as a subcontractor can be a great way to augment or expand the services you offer. Subcontractors can bring specialized skills to the table, which allows you to take on work that you may otherwise not be able to complete yourself.

salt. Because your time as a consultant is valuable, you need to weed out those people who are not qualified.

If you find applicants who are very impressive on paper, give them a telephone call and talk with them for a few minutes. Screening job applicants by phone will save you wasted hours in the long run. Before you make that telephone call, jot down a few notes and questions you should be prepared to ask, including:

1. Why do you want the job?
2. Why are you qualified to take the job?
3. What is your best quality?
4. What are your weaknesses?

Partner Perfect?

Having a business partner is similar to having a spouse. You need to make sure you and your partner agree on everything, never have any fights about money, and have the same dreams and goals. Since no marriage can ever have all the qualities we just described, how can a consultant expect to find a business partner who has them?

It can be a difficult process. If your consulting business has grown to the point where you need additional help, reconsider bringing in a partner unless you put absolutely everything in writing that each partner is responsible for. Partnerships have ended up in court because one partner accused the other of doing something wrong or of violating some partnership agreement or contract.

In the beginning, during the so-called "honeymoon period," you and your partner will have no problem getting along. In fact, you will probably begin to think, "Heck, why didn't I bring in a partner a long time ago?" Although there are exceptions to the partnership rule (and yes, some businesspeople can be partners without problems), you need to realize that at any given time, your partner could decide to pull out, set up shop for himself or herself, and literally put you out of business.

It's better to hire an associate consultant—one who works directly under you. Make sure you have a noncompete clause in your contract with your associate. (In other words, if your associate leaves your organization, he or she will be prohibited from starting a consulting business for a specific time period; the standard is 18 months.) The average pay for an associate consultant is $30,000 to $50,000 per year. Good places to look for an associate are professional associations, industry newsletters, and colleges and universities. Look for enthusiasm, critical thinking and time management skills, and make sure the candidate is a fast learner.

If after asking those four questions you feel the person may be a good candidate for your consulting business, make an appointment for an in-person interview.

Anteing Up

Although it's not necessary to divulge to your candidates how much a job pays at the first interview, it's definitely something you need to decide before you call in the reinforcements. Obviously, if you're hiring someone who will have a great deal of responsibility, like an associate who has

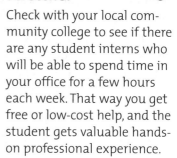

Dollar Stretcher

Check with your local community college to see if there are any student interns who will be able to spend time in your office for a few hours each week. That way you get free or low-cost help, and the student gets valuable hands-on professional experience.

virtually as much responsibility as you do, he or she should be paid more than, say, the person hired to stuff envelopes and answer your phone. By the same token, a full-time associate who has a higher level of responsibility should probably be hired as a salaried rather than an hourly employee—not so you can milk that person for a lot of overtime without pay, but because that's the more professional way of paying a valued employee.

Coming up with an equitable pay scale can be tricky. According to the *Occupational Outlook Handbook, 2004–05 Edition*, published by the U.S. Department of Labor, management analysts who consult in the management, scientific and technical fields and were employed by consulting firms earned a median hourly wage of $34.52 in 2002. (Important note: The handbook also says that self-employed consultants often earn "considerably more than the industry average.") Secretaries (except those working in the legal, medical and executive fields) earned $12.98, while office clerks earned $9.47. Obviously, these hourly wages far exceed the U.S. minimum wage, but you probably won't want to pay on the low end of the scale, even for the humblest employee. Shoot

Bright Idea

If you're reluctant to hire a secretary or word processor to keep up with the ever-increasing demands of your business, consider this: You can earn a lot more money consulting than you can typing proposals or sending out direct mail. Can't justify hiring a regular employee? Get a temp.

for a wage somewhere in between the median wages discussed above and the current minimum wage.

Don't want to try to guess what's fair? Then consider calling one of the consultant organizations listed in the Appendix and ask what the average wage is. Chances are, they've done surveys and would have that data right at hand for specific industries. Alternatively, you could ask other consultants with whom you are friendly what they're paying their staff. Most people will be happy to share this kind of information. (Just don't ask them to divulge client names.)

Fringe Benefits

If you're really going to do this employee thing right, you also need to consider offering benefits to your new staffer(s). A good benefits package is not only a powerful draw for new hires, it's also a great retention tool. Of course, there's no denying that benefits can be expensive. A recent survey by the U.S. Department of Labor's Bureau of Labor Statistics indicated that the average cost of benefits per hour is 27.9 percent, which can be prohibitive for a small-business owner. Your cost is more likely to be around 8 to 10 percent because you'll probably offer just the basics. But you'll find that offering even basic medical insurance and other benefits can help to attract better, more qualified employees.

Benefits typically offered by entrepreneurs in professional fields include:

- Group health and life insurance
- Vacation and holiday pay
- Sick pay
- Flexible hours

Other highly desirable benefits include pension plans, profit sharing plans, and Simplified Employee Pension plans. But don't worry about those particular benefits for now. You're not likely to offer this level of benefits early in your consulting career, and, frankly, just offering health insurance can be a big enough draw for employees.

Taxes

No discussion of employees would be complete without addressing the issue of payroll taxes. Employers (even those with just one employee) must withhold several different types of taxes from employees, including income tax, FICA (aka Social Security), and Medicare. It's also necessary to keep detailed records about the amounts withheld and when the funds are sent to the IRS (usually on a quarterly basis). For more information about withholding and taxes, pick up a copy of the IRS Publication 15, *Employer's Tax Guide*, as well as Publication 583, *Starting a Business and Keeping Records.* Both are available online from www.irs.gov or at your local IRS office.

Those are just the payroll taxes. As an employer, you also must pay:

- The matching portion of the FICA, or Social Security, tax, which in 2004 was 6.2 percent
- The matching portion of Medicare taxes (1.45 percent)
- State unemployment tax (the amount varies by state)

> **! Beware!**
>
> If you decide to take on a partner, make sure that any checks you write require both of your signatures. This will prevent any surprises when it comes to the financial end of your business.

- Self-employment tax on your own earnings (which is the Social Security tax on your personal earnings since you're self-employed)
- Federal Unemployment Tax, which pays for unemployment insurance programs (another 6.2 percent, or just .8 percent if you pay state unemployment insurance)
- Workers' compensation insurance (the amount varies by state)

It's almost enough to make you want to do it all alone, isn't it? But look on the bright side: If you're using a minimum wage staffer, the taxes don't amount to very much, and you can recoup the cost by building extra fees into client contracts.

8

Back to School

As you know, one of a consultant's greatest strengths is his or her knowledge of a particular industry or business. As a result, keeping abreast of changes and innovations in your field is a must if you want to be an effective advisor. One way to do this is by taking classes to update your knowledge, reading publications pertinent to your field, and joining industry-related organizations. Read on for information about the consulting organizations, publications, and certification programs that can help you stay informed and ultimately do business better. You'll find contact information for each resource discussed here, as well as others, in the Appendix.

Industry Associations

No matter which type of consultancy you're starting, from information technology to turf grass management, there's probably an association devoted exclusively to it. Space constraints don't allow us to delve into a discussion of all of those specialized organizations here, so instead here's a look at some of the broad-based organizations you may find helpful as you embark on your consulting career.

- *American Consultants League (ACL).* This organization was founded in 1983 and has lofty goals: It strives to help both beginning and experienced independent consultants earn six-figure incomes right out of the gate. Among its many member benefits are a home study course to show you how to earn $250,000 a year or more, the online Early to Rise publication and the Early to Rise monthly newsletter, a member bulletin board, a free coaching session with one of ACL's team of experts, free critiques of two of your consulting documents or promotions, and even a discounted credit card acceptance program so your clients can pay you with plastic. Its discussion forum, called "Consulting," can be found at http://speakoutforum.com. Membership is $359 annually and is offered on a risk-free trial basis.

- *Association of Professional Communication Consultants (APCC).* OK, so this is one of the more specialized organizations. But communications consulting is such a prominent field that we're including the organization here. APCC offers a wide range of benefits and resources, including promotional and marketing opportunities, seminars, e-mail discussion forums, business tools like sample proposals, and discounts on APCC publications. The organization publishes Consulting Success, an online quarterly newsletter that's included with the organization's $50 annual membership fee.

- *Association of Professional Consultants (APC).* Established to provide businesses with a resource for locating qualified consultant services, APC focuses on marketing and business practice development through referrals, networking opportunities, marketing and practice management programs, and support teams. It also offers a speakers bureau and discounts on APC business functions. Dues are $200 annually, with a one-time $75 processing fee when you join.

- *Canadian Association of Management Consultants (CAMC).* For our friends north of the border, CAMC offers professional development opportunities such as online courses, local workshops and seminars, a speakers bureau, networking opportunities, insurance programs, and more. Dues are approximately $500 annually.

- *National Association of Computer Consultant Businesses (NACCB).* We've decided to include this specialty organization on this list because IT consultants are in such high demand. This group offers various business tools, including a business owners manual, model business contracts, research, networking opportunities, education, and two quarterly publications: NACCB Monitor and Legislative & Legal Update. Annual dues are $1,000, with a one-time initiation fee of $500.

- *Professional and Technical Consultants Association (PATCA).* The wide-ranging membership of this organization includes independent consultants and principals in small firms in fields ranging from hardware and software engineering to human resources, marketing, management, and other technical and nontechnical fields. Three verifiable professional references are required with your membership application, and the annual dues for an associate membership (the category designed for consultants with less than one year of full-time consulting experience) is $395. Benefits include monthly networking meetings, free copies of the PATCA Rate Survey and PATCA Directory, a subscription to the quarterly PATCA Journal, and state legislative representation.

One more organization bears mentioning. The Institute of Management Consultants offers many resources for members, including a national conference, a certification program, a newsletter, and more. However, you must have at least five years of full-time consulting experience and a bachelor's degree to be eligible for membership. In the meantime, you might be interested in receiving the organization's quarterly magazine, *Consulting to Management*, which is discussed below.

Publications and E-Zines

Another way to stay current on news, information, events and trends in the consulting field is by subscribing to industry publications. Some you might consider include:

- *Consultants News.* Geared toward larger consulting firms, this newsletter nonetheless provides interesting reading even for fledgling consultants. Twelve print and online issues are $349 a year, and the subscription includes online archive access and e-mail alerts. You can try a free issue by calling (800) 531-0007 or (603) 924-0900, ext. 773, or e-mailing CNsample@kennedyinfo.com. It's published by market research firm Kennedy Information Inc., which also publishes *Consulting Magazine*. The latter is sent

Dollar Stretcher

You can deduct the cost of professional publications on your business income taxes. Be sure to retain a copy of your canceled check or an invoice paid in full with your tax records as proof of payment.

free of charge to consultants making the really big bucks (as in seven figures). But you can subscribe for $99 a year until you hit that benchmark. Recent article topics included finding a mentor, finding the best places to stay, and charting career changes.

- *Consulting Wire.* A free e-newsletter from Kennedy Information Inc. with commentary on news concerning the consulting industry. Subscribe at http://register .consultingcentral.com.

- *Consulting to Management.* A publication of the Institute of Management Consultants USA, this quarterly magazine's mission is to develop, collect, and publish the growing body of knowledge within the consulting fields, both as a profession and as a business. The annual subscription is $80, or $100 for an electronic subscription.

- *Inside Consulting.* Written by Tom Rodenhauser, president of market research and advisory firm Consulting Information Services LLC, this free e-mail column addresses issues of interest to the management consulting and IT services industries. Subscribe at www.consultinginfo.com/subscribe.asp.

> ## Bright Idea
> In addition to subscribing to publications relevant to your area of expertise, you should be a regular reader of publications like *The Wall Street Journal, Fortune,* and *BusinessWeek* to help keep you abreast of changes and trends in the business world that can impact your consultancy.

Certification

Certification from a recognized consulting organization can enhance your reputation and increase your credibility, although in most cases, you must be a practicing consultant for a period of several years (usually five) before you can become certified. You can earn certifications from the American Consultants League, the Institute of Management Consultants, and the National Bureau of Certified Consultants Inc. The latter is an independent organization founded in 1989 and devoted solely to the business of certifying consultants who have a bachelor's degree and at least five years of full-time or ten years of part-time consulting experience. Consultants with less than five years' experience are eligible for membership in the AAPC Division/American Association of Professional Consultants.

> ## Bright Idea
> Pursuing a general business education (or an MBA if you already hold an undergraduate degree) can really give you an edge in your profession. Coursework in marketing, public relations, organizational change, and finance can be particularly useful.

For Further Study

In addition to becoming certified, consultants can expand their knowledge base by seeking more formalized education. The National Bureau of Certified Consultants sponsors two educational paths: a self-study program called "Complete Consulting Success," which leads to a certificate in the Principles of Consulting to Management; and a self-study course for consultants doing business in the global digital economy, for which participants earn a certificate in e-business and e-commerce from the Complete-21 Institute for Digital Commerce.

Finally, some universities offer certificates in consultancy through their extended learning or continuing education departments. Among them are San Diego State University's College of Extended Studies and the Georgia Center for Continuing Education. You might try contacting your local university or community college to find out if they offer similar programs.

You don't have to spend big bucks to improve your skills as a consultant or small-business owner. As mentioned earlier, many professional and service organizations offer seminars in various topics of interest to their members, so it pays to keep an eye on their special event calendars to catch their no- or low-cost workshops.

The SCORE Corps

Imagine a resource that helps you build business, provides current resources, and connects you with business professionals who can dispense advice and wisdom—and all at no charge. You get all that and more from SCORE, a nationwide association of retired and working volunteers, entrepreneurs, and corporate managers/executives.

Known as the "Counselors to America's Small Business," this resource partner of the SBA boasts 389 chapters nationwide that offer free one-on-one counseling to entrepreneurs, as well as no- or low-cost workshops on everything from entrepreneurship, to marketing, to public relations, and more.

"After the workshops, you can grab a counselor and ask specific questions," says Merrily Schiavone, a Newark, Delaware, consultant. "SCORE is just wonderful."

The organization's web site (www.score.org) also is a treasure trove of information. In addition to offering free e-zines, the site has a Business Toolbox with business document templates, a marketing workbook, online workshops, and much more.

To contact SCORE, call (800) 634-0245.

Getting the Word Out

Now that you have the basic structure of your new business established or at least under construction, it's time to start marketing your services and capabilities to potential clients. After all, if your consulting business has no clients, then you have no consulting business. But you must remember that selling your consulting services is not the same as selling a car or a house. In the case of the car or the house, the customer is probably already in the market for one or both of those products. Your job is harder because you are marketing your services to people who may not even be aware they need those services.

There are a variety of methods you need to become both familiar and comfortable with to begin getting the word out about your business. Let's look at some of the more conventional ones that are being used by many consultants today.

Direct Mail

Anyone who is seriously considering starting a consulting business had better know at least the basics of direct mail. With direct mail, you simply send your prospective clients a brochure, flier, or letter describing the consulting services you offer.

It's not that hard to come up with an award-winning direct-mail campaign. In fact, if you think about it, you are already an expert in the direct-mail field. When you get home from a hard day at the office and the mail is tossed onto the kitchen table or counter, what process do you use to sort through it? If you are like most people, you pull out the bills, set them aside, then look to see if any personal letters or cards have arrived. Then and only then do you begin to look through the junk mail. That's right, every direct-mail piece will sooner or later be classified as junk mail—even the ones you crafted so carefully. So don't take it personally; it's just a fact of life.

When you come across an interesting piece of direct mail, you open it to see what exciting offers are hidden inside. What motivated you to open the envelope—even though you knew it was just another attempt to sell you something? It's important to understand that motivation because in the exciting world of direct mail, getting someone to open the envelope is half the battle. So now you know why businesses, government agencies, nonprofit organizations—virtually anyone with anything to sell via direct mail—invest so much time and expense designing just the right "sell piece."

It may not be rocket science to put a winning direct-mail piece together, but it sure helps to understand the parts and process. To illustrate, let's say you go to a bookstore to look around, but you don't have a particular title in mind to buy. So what do you do? You probably first spend some time browsing, looking for something that jumps off the shelf and says "Buy me!" Publishers who go the extra mile doing market research into what makes consumers pick up a book know the importance of having just the right color and design on the cover and the right

> ## Bright Idea
> Ask your friends, neighbors, and business associates to save any direct-mail pieces they have found interesting and that compelled them to open the envelope. Start a file and save them; review the file at least twice a year.

Sample Direct-Mail Letter

September 12, 200X

Dear Executive Director,

Did you know that in the next 90 days more than $10 million will be donated to nonprofit agencies in Delaware by local foundations? Do you know how to apply for your fair share of these funds?

My name is John Riddle, and I have more than ten years' experience as a fundraising professional. I have worked at nonprofit agencies in Delaware, Maryland and Pennsylvania as a development director, director of special events, and vice president of public relations.

If you need temporary fundraising help for a day, a week, or a few months, call on an experienced fundraising professional to help you meet your fundraising goal. Why not give me a call today? Together we can develop a plan of action that will work for your agency.

Sincerely,

John Riddle

John Riddle
Fundraising Consultant

Brochure Basics

Your brochure should include these five elements:

1. It should clearly convey what your services are.

2. It should tell customers why you are the best.

3. It should give a few reasons why you should be hired.

4. It should include some brief biographical information.

5. It should include some information about who your other clients are.

That's it. Keep it simple, but do it right. Remember, your brochure represents you in the marketplace, so make sure you polish it before you send it into action. Your entire consulting career depends on it.

---

copy inside the jacket. Those are the important features consumers look for when they are shopping for a new book, and you'll find they're the same types of features readers look for when they receive direct-mail pieces.

When you receive something in the mail that screams "Open me!" then the writer, designer, and graphic artist have done their jobs. So now you know you need to have a dynamite direct-mail piece advertising your consulting business and services.

If writing the perfect brochure or direct-mail letter scares the daylights out of you, hire a professional writer. A really good direct-mail piece is worth its weight in gold. So don't cut corners when it comes time to do yours! For inspiration, see page 69 for a sample brochure and page 67 for a sample direct-mail letter.

Cold Calls

If the thought of making cold calls gives you the shivers, then you'd better hire someone to do your marketing for you because it's that important. But relax, making cold calls can be fun; it all depends on your attitude. But even if you're not exactly jumping for joy at this aspect of marketing, it will pay to learn as much about successful cold calling as you possibly can.

First, be prepared to be rejected. It's nothing personal; it's just the way things work. Say you decide on a Monday morning to begin your day by making cold calls to obtain the clients you need to keep your business in a healthy cash-flow situation. To get at least

Sample Brochure

Inside Flap	Back Cover	Front Cover

L R S MARKETING

GOES TO WORK AS YOUR:

◆ Project Planner
◆ Document Designer
◆ Writer
◆ Artist
◆ Publicity Partner
◆ Quality Assurance Team

We will be there for you!

L R S MARKETING INC.

L R S MARKETING INC.

MARKETING/
ADVERTISING
CONSULTANTS

"Reach For The Stars"

Tel: 302-994-2147

Inside Spread

ABOUT US...

L R S Marketing Inc. was founded in 1996. Its staff has over 23 years of marketing and advertising experience.

Since its founding in 1996, L R S Marketing has been devoted to upgrading the quality of marketing and advertising in this highly competitive market.

When you hire L R S Marketing, you're hiring a ready-made team of specialists that can make a difference in your business. All the components are in place: project manager, copy writers, editor, media and advertising consultants.

We hire experience, and all of us are great fun to work with.

Let L R S Marketing assist you in all the phases of marketing your company or products.

"Gentlemen start your engins"

WHAT WE DO...

We will meet with you to assure your comfort and satisfaction. Together with you, we create marketing and advertising that is unique, personal and profitable. We become involved in every aspect of the planning to provide you with the personal attention you deserve. L R S Marketing provides an invaluable service to companies. As full-time consultants, we concentrate on your needs. We have creativity, organizational skills and a very professional approach. These qualities are necessary to create the perfect plan!

"Golf with the Masters"

Project Planning And Management

We plan your documents, analyze the audience needs, define its contents, generate outlines, design the document, as well as schedule and budget the project.

Writing

L R S Marketing writes the drafts, revises text, incorporates review comments, writes the final draft and sends it off to the printer.

Editing

We edit the text for consistency, accuracy and usability. L R S will assist with preparing your artwork and integrating it with your text.

"And they're off"

Quality Assurance

We test your documents for accuracy and completeness.

L R S MARKETING INC.

1915 East Zabenko Drive
Wilmington, DE 19808
Phone: 302-994-2147
Fax: 302-994-2147
Email: Roxy1102@aol.com

one prospect to say "yes," you may have to make between 20 and 30 contacts with people who have the authority to hire you.

Yes, you read that correctly. To get at least one "yes," you will have to experience an awful lot of "nos." Depending on your fee schedule, that figure could be even higher—or possibly lower. To increase the chances of getting more "yes" responses, you must be flexible with your rates. In other words, do whatever it takes to grab that client, even if it means taking less money for the job. After all, that work could lead to repeat business or word-of-mouth referrals, which make that initial reduction in fees a lot easier to accept.

By the way, if you really hate making cold calls, you should know you're not alone. Merrily Schiavone, a Newark, Delaware, consultant, is an experienced cold caller who once sold advertising. Yet she, too, dislikes picking up the phone and prospecting for work from people she doesn't know.

"I prefer to be in a situation where someone knows who I am, which is why I like networking instead," she says. "With networking, the people you meet typically are ready to request your services, and I get a lot of business that way. But cold calling is a necessary part of doing business that everyone needs to do."

What can you do to make the cold-calling process easier? To begin with, try phoning business contacts between the hours of 6 and 8:30 A.M. A lot of people arrive at the office early to catch up on work before the pressures of a normal day start mounting, so it can be a great time to catch someone when he or she might be more receptive to your sales pitch. Second, practice your pitch, both out loud and in front of a supportive business colleague or friend. Ask for feedback on the effectiveness and the sincerity of your delivery, and make adjustments as necessary. Finally, set goals for yourself—say, two cold calls made twice a week. We guarantee that the more you call, the easier it will become—and you might even land some new business along the way.

John Riddle, a Bear, Delaware, consultant, has pretty much mastered the art of cold calling, but he, too, has had to eat some costs to make a sale. When he was working as a fundraising consultant, for instance, he published a series of fundraising newsletters for the nonprofit industry. Every month, the newsletters had just one page of advertising for fundraising products and services of interest to people and organizations intent on raising money for various causes.

Riddle's usual way of soliciting advertising clients was via direct mail, and most months, he

> **Beware!**
> Be sensitive to what time of day you make any cold calls. Never call at dinnertime, and be aware of any difference in time zones. If you're not sure which time zone you're calling, plug the area code into an internet browser like Google, and voilà, you'll know whether you're calling Michigan or Montana.

Warming Up to Cold Calls

There are a few tricks you can use to make cold-calling a little easier:

○ *Prepare a script ahead of time.* Spell out word for word what you expect to say when you get someone on the telephone. Remember, though, that your goal is to get a face-to-face interview and, eventually, a new client. So before you end up stumbling over your sales presentation (either in person or over the telephone), write your script and practice it again and again.

○ *Be creative in your efforts to reach the decision maker.* Most times you will encounter a secretary or administrative assistant who has years of experience turning away cold callers like yourself. But don't give up. (One of Winston Churchill's favorite sayings was "Never give up, never give up, never ever give up!" It's good advice.) To avoid being screened by the secretary, try calling before she is on the job. You may have to call before 8 A.M. or after 5 P.M., but at these times, chances are the decision makers you are trying to reach will answer their own telephones.

○ *Limit your cold calls to just several days each month.* And make sure you put your best effort into the process. That way, not only will it become easier to make those cold calls, but you will find yourself actually looking forward to making them.

had no trouble selling enough ads to fill the page. But on occasion, he would have to hustle and sell those ads by making cold calls.

The most effective pitch he ever made entailed telling potential customers there was only one quarter-page ad left and that the usual selling price for an ad of that size was $400. Then he would floor customers by saying they could name their own price for the space. Some people would pass on that incredible offer, but most could not resist, and the average offer he received for the space was $250 to $350. One potential advertiser offered a mere $25 for the ad space, but when Riddle asked him if that's all he thought his product was worth, he ended up making a better offer.

Advertising

Because advertising can be very expensive, it's important to spend your advertising dollars wisely. Jeffery Bartlett, a Harrisburg, Pennsylvania, marketing research consultant, maximizes his advertising dollars by advertising only in his association's publication. "The association publishes what is called the Green Book, which is a directory of research and marketing consulting businesses around the country," he says. "It has helped me generate new business." Other consultants, such as Schiavone, depend on word-of-mouth. "The best form of advertising [for my business] has been word-of-mouth and recommendations from other people," she says. "I've found that being active in organizations like the chamber of commerce generates a lot of leads."

You may find that all you have to do to get your business rolling is to advertise early on in your new career. "When I started out, I wanted to work in the nonprofit field so I initially did some advertising," says Bill Metten, a Hockessin, Delaware, public relations consultant. "But I wasn't after high-profile clients, and the state is so small that everyone knows everyone else. So now I rely on word-of-mouth to land new business."

Dollar Stretcher

Contact publications that are directed at your target audience to see if they have any special advertising sections scheduled for production in the next few months. They almost always do, and they may have special discount advertising rates. This is particularly true when it comes to trade newspapers and journals.

Depending upon the type of services you offer, it may be necessary to advertise in specialized trade journals or magazines. Before you spend any money on this, though, start looking through back issues of professional journals and newspapers related to the fields you specialize in. If you don't subscribe to those journals or newspapers, visit your nearest university or college library since chances are good they'll have them in their collection. Note how many times other consultants have placed those ads. What type of ads did they use? Did they place large display ads? Or did they limit themselves to smaller ads in the publications' classified sections? Do they use clip art, or are they all type? How effective are the ads, in your opinion?

After examining these materials, you can start making decisions about your own advertising efforts. Feel free to adapt the best ideas for use in your ads. Just be careful not to plagiarize anyone else's work.

In addition to placing ads in the full print run of a publication, you also should consider advertising in any specialty sections that might include a "Consultants Directory" or "Directory of Consulting Services." (Consulting professionals such as Riddle stress that directory advertising is well worth the cost.) To find out if your target publication plans to produce a directory of consulting services, contact its advertising department and ask for an editorial calendar. Keep in mind, though, that publications can have lead times of as much as six months, so be sure to call for a copy of the editorial calendar no later than August or September if you think you'd like to advertise during the following year.

Another expensive yet effective way of advertising is in your local Yellow Pages. To determine whether you should advertise, take a look at your own local telephone book to see what types of consultants have already placed ads there. Better yet, when you are at the library looking through back issues of those professional publications, take some time and browse through some telephone books from other cities (you can usually find a large collection of telephone books in the reference section). Again, take a look at the different ads and listings in the Yellow Pages that feature consultants and consulting services.

When you first opened a page that listed consultants, did your eyes go directly to the display ads, which are the largest ads on the page? Probably so. That's what a display ad is supposed to do—catch your eye and say, "Hey, read me first!" The psychology is simple. A larger ad will attract more potential clients than a regular classified listing ever will. And people may assume that since you have spent extra money on that display ad, you may be more established and even more professional than those consultants who did not opt for the large ad. If your budget permits, experiment with different sizes of display ads and see which one draws in the most business.

If you can't afford to do this kind of experimentation (and many newbies can't), remember that it's entirely possible to create an effective small-space ad.

There is one caveat when it comes to Yellow Pages advertising. There are so many phone companies these days, each with their own directories, that it can be difficult to know which one to choose.

"I think the usefulness of a Yellow Pages ad is directly related to geography," says Huntington Beach, California, consultant Susan Bock. "In a smaller area, it might be useful. But if your area has different service providers and each city has its own phone book, it can be hard to justify the cost of advertising in all of them."

Newsletters

Newsletters can be a very effective tool when it comes to drumming up clients for your consulting business. Through newsletters, you can present news of interest to potential clients and remind former clients that you are still alive and kicking—and available if they need help again.

When Riddle started as a fundraising consultant, it became clear to him that publishing a variety of fundraising newsletters was the most effective means he could possibly use to sign up new clients. So Riddle began mailing a free six-month subscription to local nonprofit agencies he thought might benefit the most from his newsletter and might be good candidates to use his consulting services. Because he controlled the articles that appeared in each issue, he could use the space to tell of successes he had achieved as a fundraising consultant for other nonprofits.

His strategy paid off. Within the first year, Riddle received consulting contracts from four nonprofit organizations—all because they had been on his free mailing list. And this is a strategy you can use, too. Newsletters are usually four pages long, which gives you plenty of room to experiment with different types of articles that subtly sell your services while providing information the reader can use.

> **Smart Tip** Tip...
>
> If you need to hire a freelance writer, contact your local newspaper to see if there are any writing clubs or associations that meet in your area. You could also check the various writing web sites on the internet; they will be a valuable resource if you need professional writing assistance.

If you work in a technical field like computer consulting, a newsletter can be a smart way to showcase your knowledge—and generate new business. For instance, David McMullen, a Costa Mesa, California, computer consultant, e-mails a two-page newsletter to a list of about 350 clients and prospects. It's full of tips for fixing problems or working more efficiently, plus it serves as a reminder to anyone who hasn't used his services for a while to call if they have a technology problem.

Whatever your consulting field is, you should have more than enough information to produce a newsletter that can be used to attract potential clients. If you don't have the time or don't feel comfortable self-publishing your newsletter, hire a local freelance

Anatomy of a Newsletter

A typical newsletter published by a consultant will include:

○ *News of importance to the industry.* You can collect information from a variety of sources, including magazines, newspapers, professional journals, web sites, etc. Just make sure you credit the source of each news item you use.

○ *Editorials and opinions.* Here is your chance to sound off on a particular subject relative to your consulting field.

○ *Tips for success.* Tell your readers how they can do their jobs better.

writer and graphic designer to do the job for you. It doesn't have to be an expensive, four-color, glossy publication. In fact, the simpler it is, the better. A good newsletter will sell itself based on the content rather than on a splashy design.

To get some ideas, start collecting newsletters published in your field. If you're not familiar with any, make a quick visit to your local library and look for a copy of the *Oxbridge Directory of Newsletters* (Oxbridge Communications) and *Hudson's Subscription Newsletter Directory* (The Newsletter Clearinghouse), which list by subject newsletters published both in the United States and other countries. Then write or e-mail the publishers of newsletters you're interested in and ask for sample copies before you design and write your first issue. You'll be surprised at the quality of the newsletters that are being produced today.

Don't underestimate the power of a newsletter. Last time you received one in the mail, did you put it aside to read later? And why did you do that? Probably because you wanted to make sure you weren't missing any important news or information. And what about that brochure you received in the mail the same day? Did you put it aside to read later or did it go directly into the trash can? Think about that before you spend big bucks on a glitzy brochure that may not even be read.

Referrals

This often-overlooked method of finding new clients is such an easy marketing tool you just may kick yourself for not thinking of it yourself. All you have to do is wait until you have finished your consulting assignment and your client is in seventh heaven, then ask for a referral. Rather than putting your client on the spot, just send a note or a short letter to him or her asking for the names of any colleagues, friends, or business associates who might be good prospects for your consulting services. Chances are good you'll get some excellent leads, as David McMullen has discovered. He even goes so far as to tell each client that referrals are his only source of new business and that he would be very appreciative if they passed his name on to someone who could use his services. "If everyone I know sent me one name," he says, "I'd have more work than I'd know what to do with."

It's also a nice idea to send a letter to clients on their birthdays—or any other noteworthy occasion—to wish them a happy day and remind them that you appreciate their business and are available for additional work. There's a sample special occasion letter on page 76 you can adapt for your own use.

A simple thank-you letter can be your best friend in the consulting business. For a sample, turn to page 77. There's nothing better than a client who remembers you fondly and feels that you really did the best job you could—and a thank-you letter helps them do just that.

Sample Special Occasion Letter

MARKETING INC.
1000 East Culver Drive
Wilmington, CA 90006
Phone: (949) 857-2000
e-mail: LRSmarketing@aol.com

February 11, 200X

Robin Proctor
Alarm Data Corp.
2500 Eastburn Drive
Irvine, CA 19000

Dear Robin,

Happy birthday!

Please accept our wishes for an enjoyable day and a prosperous year.

We also want to take this opportunity to thank you for your business. Customers like you make it all worthwhile.

Congratulations again,

R.S Walker

R.S. Walker
President
LRS Marketing Inc.

MARKETING INC.

1000 East Culver Drive
Wilmington, CA 90006
Phone: (949) 857-2000
e-mail: LRSmarketing@aol.com

February 11, 200X

Randy Reed
ADT Security Service Inc.
18 Boulder Street
Tustin, CA 19720

Dear Randy,

Thank you for participating in the Home Show at the Concord Mall on May 20-23 and for choosing to do business with LRS Marketing Inc.

Our goal is to serve clients to the best of our ability. If we find more opportunities for your company to exhibit its product, we will be sure to notify you.

Thank you again for selecting us. It is our privilege to work with you.

Sincerely,

R.S Walker

R.S. Walker
President
LRS Marketing Inc.

Pressing
Business

As you already know from Chapter 9, there are a lot of things you can do to advertise your business, from sending out direct-mail pieces to cold-calling. But another way to start spreading the news about your services and capabilities is through shameless self-promotion. What we're talking about here is pure publicity, which involves telling prospective clients about who you are and what you can do for them through networking, public speaking, teaching workshops, and getting news articles out about yourself in print media (newspapers, magazines, trade journals, newsletters, etc.), or in broadcast media (TV, radio, etc.). The sky is the limit when it comes to getting publicity. In fact, you are limited only by your imagination.

Networking remains one of the best ways to generate positive word-of-mouth advertising. But until you can develop your own contacts and get that buzz working for you, you may want to try one or more of the following public relations tools.

News Releases

With the proper care and feeding of the local news media, you will be able to get the publicity you need to keep your consulting business in the black. In both print and broadcast media, editors have space they need to fill each day. Give them something they can use, and you could find yourself in print or on the air on a regular basis.

One of the simplest and most cost-effective forms of publicity at your disposal is the news release. Also known as a press release, these one- to two-page documents are sent out by companies and business professionals to tell the world about their new products and services, as well as to remind everyone how good they are at what they do. In a way, they're little advertisements for your business, except they don't cost you a thing beyond the time it takes to write them and any necessary production expenses such as stationery, envelopes, and postage. And since many editors prefer to receive releases by e-mail these days, they're about as close to free as you can get.

Generally speaking, newspaper and magazine editors use news releases as filler material. They also use them as idea starters that can be developed into related or more detailed stories. Because news releases are used on a space-available basis, there's no guarantee that yours will get into print. But that doesn't mean you shouldn't keep trying, because when one does hit print, the evening TV news, or drive-time radio, it's totally free publicity.

Even if you're not a writer by trade, you can put together a simple news release. To start the process, think about the six questions a journalist asks: Who, what, where, when, why, and how. Jot down your thoughts related to each of those questions, then choose the most important thing you want the reader to know. That becomes the lead for the release, and it's important to put this main point upfront since editors tend to cut copy from the end of a release if it's too long to run in its entirety. Then fill in with other important details, and you're good to go.

Media Lists

If you're just starting in the consulting business, it will be worth your while to obtain the editorial calendars and contact lists for your local media. This way, when you're ready to send something to the press, you have the name of the reporter or editor you need to contact. (Make a quick telephone call to the source to make sure the contact name has not changed. It's not unusual to find that an editor has either moved on to a new assignment or has left that organization altogether.)

The easiest way to build a list is to use a web site like www.mondotimes.com, which lists all the print, TV, and radio outlets in your community. With this information in hand, you can obtain contact info on each media outlet via the internet. You may also have to call to obtain the

Smart Tip

Check with your local media contacts to see if they prefer to have news releases and public service announcements sent via e-mail, fax, or snail mail. By working with the media on their terms, you are enhancing your chances of getting the coverage you desire.

name of the editor or assignment editor who would be the recipient of your releases. Additional sources for media lists are your local chamber of commerce or the department of tourism (also known as the convention and visitors bureau in some states).

Keep in mind there are some important publications that do not appear on standard media lists; namely, corporate and business newsletters. Virtually all large companies publish some type of internal employee newsletter or bulletin. (Check with the human resources departments of the companies you are targeting to see if they have such publications.) In addition to featuring news and information of interest to their employees, most of these publications also include community news and a calendar of events.

Here's a story about how company publications helped John Riddle when he worked as a fundraising consultant in Bear, Delaware. A client hired him to produce a special event he had dreamed up: an attempt to make the Guinness Book of World Records by having the largest group of people ever dance the Twist at one time. Since at that time there was no category for doing the Twist, the Guinness people said there had to be at least 5,001 people dancing at one time to be in the record book.

Bright Idea

You can save money on the cost of producing a client newsletter by having a desktop publishing designer create a simple two-page newsletter template in a program like Microsoft Publisher, then simply plugging in the text and/or photographs yourself when you're ready to publish a new edition.

The idea was to charge people $5 and have them come to a local racetrack and enjoy music, food, and fun in a picnic grove. People were encouraged to buy their tickets ahead of time, and before long, advance ticket sales were going strong.

While local newspapers and radio stations gave the event some coverage a few days before the event, Riddle had enormous success from the press releases and stories he submitted to various corporate newsletters in town. His client began getting calls from those corporate employees who wanted to volunteer for their organization not only at that event, but also at future ones as well. The corporations also bought large blocks of tickets (at $5 each) to distribute to their employees. As a result, the event was a huge hit all around.

When Things Go Wrong

Most of the time your contact with the media will be positive, as in the story above. But if you ever have a problem with a client (or even with your own consulting business), you may find yourself dealing with the media in less desirable

Beware!
If you make a mistake that results in a missed deadline or poor performance on the job, don't try to sidestep blame. Admit your culpability, apologize, and ask how you can rectify the situation. Then do whatever it takes to make the client happy, even if it means putting in extra time on the job without payment. It's the best way to negate bad publicity.

circumstances. In that case, it's best not to avoid the media or sidestep their questions. The more you avoid them, the worse it will be, and the fallout from even the smallest hint of scandal can spell disaster. You want to avoid being the lead story on page one or on the six o'clock news because people tend to remember bad stories.

With this in mind, you should have a disaster plan ready to use in the event something goes wrong. Here are some guidelines you can use to help deflect unexpected bad press:

- Always keep the media well informed of all developments in a story.
- Don't make the media wait for answers to their questions; they may find their own sources for answers, and those other sources may not be accurate.
- Use only facts. Do not give theories, conjecture, or anything else besides the facts.
- Update information as often as possible.
- Maintain a professional attitude.
- Have just one person in charge (most likely) to be responsible for answering questions from reporters.

Public Speaking

Public speaking is another excellent way to recruit new clients and to earn a reputation for excellence in your community. Unless you live in a town so small it doesn't have a chamber of commerce or a Lions Club, Rotary Club, or other similar service organization, you can begin offering your services as a speaker for luncheons, dinners, or any other special occasion.

Susan Bock, a Huntington Beach, California, human resources consultant, does a lot of public speaking for professional organizations on topics ranging from empowerment and team building to organizational effectiveness, interviewing techniques and diversity training. In addition to delivering her wisdom to groups as small as a dozen people and as large as several hundred, Bock also uses the occasions to prospect for new clients.

"I leave materials on each of the tables that include a biography tailored to the audience and an invitation for a free consultation," she says. "Take-away materials like these are crucial because many of these talks are scheduled during evening meetings when people are tired after a long day at the office. If they have something to take away with them, they're more likely to call at a future time."

Riddle also has used his experience as a public speaker to land new clients. As a fundraising consultant, he often was asked to speak to organizations about the successful projects for which he has raised money. On several occasions, there were people in the audience who were volunteers or board members from other nonprofit organizations, and when the function was over, they approached him about working as a consultant for their agency.

> **Tip...**
>
> **Smart Tip**
> Service organizations that are always looking for public speakers include:
>
> - ○ American Legion
> - ○ Lions Club
> - ○ Rotary Club
> - ○ Kiwanis Club
> - ○ Chambers of commerce
> - ○ Elks Lodge
> - ○ Masons
> - ○ YMCA/YWCA
> - ○ PTA organizations
> - ○ VFW chapters

So unless you are deathly afraid of public speaking (and you'd better not be, because as a consultant, you will be presenting oral and written reports for your clients), get busy and start contacting those local service organizations. To find them, use the telephone directory and ask around to find out if anyone has published a directory of service organizations in your community. You also can visit the library and ask at the reference desk. Go through and make a list of organizations that hold monthly meetings and therefore may use guest speakers. Contact each group and offer your services.

Teaching a Workshop

One sure-fire way to discover if the field you have chosen is one in which you will succeed is to put together enough material to teach a workshop. It doesn't have to be anything fancy—just a talk that will hold people's attention and give them some good information in your area of expertise.

It's possible to turn any topic, interest, or specialty into a workshop, as Riddle discovered. Although he had no real teaching experience, he felt compelled to share his experiences as a freelance writer with other people who were trying to break into that field. He had struggled for nearly five years without successfully publishing anything,

Hitting the Lecture Circuit

Making contact with organizations and associations that would be interested in having you address their monthly membership meetings or other special events is just the first step in landing speaking engagements that can increase your visibility. It's also a good idea to come up in advance with several viable lecture topics to pitch to those groups, as well as any handouts or other materials you might like to distribute. That way, you'll be ready on a moment's notice to fill a vacant slot on a meeting agenda.

Because there are bound to be people in the audience who either could use someone with your particular expertise or who know someone else who's looking for a consultant, be sure to tell the audience during your presentation that you're a consultant in the (fill-in-the-blank) field, then use examples and stories in your talk directly related to your field. Also, always take a generous supply of your business cards and brochures along with you and leave them on the table next to the podium where you're speaking. Anyone who comes up to speak to you afterward will certainly pick them up.

even though he had read every book he could find on the subject and attended a few workshops for beginning writers.

Then one day he read an article in *Writer's Digest* magazine about how newspapers and magazines were always on the lookout for freelance writers to write book reviews. The article took him step-by-step through the process of getting his first book review published. And much to his surprise, the advice worked. Within a few weeks of reading that article (which he now uses as a handout in his writing workshops), his first book review was published, and it opened up many other publishing opportunities.

So Riddle decided to offer a workshop for beginning freelance writers, which he called "Introduction to Freelance Writing." He contacted a local school district to see if there was any interest in including the workshop in the fall catalog of noncredit courses it was offering to adults in the evening hours. They were delighted and asked him to submit a course description the next day.

After carefully reviewing his files (which were filled with nearly 20 years' worth of writing advice), Riddle came up with a course outline and found out that he had more material than he could ever use. So the point is: If you are both passionate and knowledgeable about your chosen consulting field, you should be able and willing to present a workshop on it. And you just might meet people in your workshop who one day could use your consulting services or will refer you to someone else who can. Plus the added visibility is always a good thing for your business. So try developing a workshop—it could be your ticket to increased profit.

The Importance of Associations

If you expect to do business in your community, consider joining one or more professional business organizations. These groups provide you with opportunities to meet other members (some of whom may need your services), serve on committees, and otherwise gain visibility and credibility among business acquaintances. Among the organizations that have excellent networking potential are the chamber of commerce, the Rotary Club, and any local economic development group.

"Networking is a real art, and many chambers of commerce hold seminars to teach you how to do it," says Newark, Delaware, consultant Merrily Schiavone. "They teach you how to ask the right questions, pitch your own company in 30 seconds, and know when to move on if it doesn't look like your services will be needed. A new consultant will find this information very valuable."

Riddle has used his memberships in professional associations to great advantage. As a member of the National Society of Fund Raising Executives and the Delaware Association of Nonprofit Agencies, he was able to keep in touch with the majority of the people and nonprofit agencies within the state of Delaware, and just by developing this network of contacts and attending various luncheons and other events, he obtained plenty of contracts.

Melinda Patrician, a consultant in Arlington, Virginia, also believes that it's important to network with associations in your field. "As a public relations consultant who has done work for many book publishers, I keep in touch with people in the industry," she says.

The point is, you can't just sit in your office, send out brochures and expect people to beat down your door. You need to get out and be with people—especially those who could use your consulting services.

Bright Idea

Check the calendar section of your local newspaper and magazines, which usually lists clubs and organizations that are having meetings and luncheons. A telephone number and a contact name will probably be listed, too, so take advantage of this free resource.

To find out which associations have a chapter in your city or town, check your local library, which should have a copy of the *Encyclopedia of Associations* (Gale Research Co.). Believe it or not, there is an association for just about every activity and interest. Browse through the listings, which are alphabetized by association as well as grouped by subject matter, and copy down names and telephone numbers of the ones you would like to contact. Then follow through and sign up with the organizations that interest you most. If you come across an association that does not have a group meeting where you live, you might consider starting a local chapter. What better way to attract potential clients?

Of course, the whole point of joining organizations is to network with other business professionals at group functions. So when you arrive for a luncheon meeting or other event, circulate widely and pass out your business card every time you make a new acquaintance. But don't just blatantly come out and say you're looking for new business ("Hi, my name is Veronica Banish. I'm an image consultant and you look like you could really use help picking your wardrobe. Call me."). Rather, introduce yourself and mention what you do. Then stick to the kind of small talk you'd exchange at a cocktail party.

> **Tip...**
>
> **Smart Tip**
>
> A great way to position yourself as a specialist in your field is to sign up with ProfNet, an online network of business professionals who wish to be contacted by journalists looking for expert commentary. For a fee, ProfNet will post your biography and forward media inquiries from reporters looking for sources. For more information, go to www.profnet.com.

If the conversation turns to business, so much the better. Then you can commiserate about small-business issues like tax rates, or hiring difficulties, or time management challenges. The idea is to lay the groundwork for future business relationships, since after you see the same people a few times, they'll know who you are and probably will be inclined to call you when the need for your type of service arises.

Finally, keep an eye out for special networking meetings held by organizations like the Chamber of Commerce. The sole purpose of these types of meetings is to get people together to exchange information and business cards, so you don't have to be shy about self-promotion. Just keep in mind that everyone else there will be doing the same thing, which can be counterproductive if you're trying to network at a meeting comprised solely of, say, computer consultants or communication consultants. In essence, you'll be networking with your competitors, who are unlikely to use your services or refer you to someone else. So your time will probably be better spent elsewhere.

11

Casting
Your Net

Unless you've been off communing with nature in the Ural Mountains for the past decade or so, chances are you're well-acquainted with the wonders of the World Wide Web, aka the internet. The internet can be a great resource for you as a consultant, both as a medium for conducting your own research for client projects and as a way for prospects to reach you.

However, although it may eventually make sense to develop a web site for your consulting business, don't rush into this venture just for the sake of saying "Yes, I'm on the internet." Rather, decide first who you're trying to reach with your web site, then consider whether this is the best way to reach prospects. Unless the clients you are trying to reach are online, you are wasting your time and money.

Test the Waters

To get an idea of whether or not you should be on the internet, spend some time looking at what other consultants have done with their web sites. Just type a term like "management consultant" or "computer consultant" into a search engine like Google and you'll get plenty of web sites to choose from. (A recent search on "management consultant" yielded more than 12 million hits, while "management consultant Detroit" resulted in 399,000 matches!) To narrow down the field and yield more relevant information, try picking the names of a few of your competitors from the local phone book and look them up instead. You're likely to discover some of your competitors have multipage web sites with company information, a client list, and more, while others have just a noninteractive "business card" web site that gives basic contact information only.

Still others such as Merrily Schiavone in Newark, Delaware, use their web sites as a portfolio of their work. "I often direct prospects who contact me for information or a quote to my web site so they can see what type of work I've done," Schiavone says. "In fact, sometimes when I'm on the phone with prospective clients, I tell them to log on so we can both look at the same sample while we're talking. Clients like having that option very much."

What you choose to do with your web site will depend on your goals and requirements. Since a certain amount of experimentation is inevitable, you might want to start off with one of the free pages available on the internet (good ones to try can be found at www.angelfire.lycos.com or http://geocities.sbc.yahoo.com). In addition, your local ISP may give you a certain amount of free web space (typically 10MB) as part of your monthly contract. It pays to ask, and it's a great way to test whether your web site really is of any value to your business.

John Riddle, in Bear, Delaware, found out the hard way the value of test marketing a web site. When he decided to sell a fundraising plan he called the "No Go, No Show" campaign, he designed several greeting cards that nonprofit

Smart Tip

Tip...

Research shows that 85 percent of internet traffic comes from a search engine, so you should register your web site on as many search engines as possible. (Popular choices are Google, Yahoo, and Lycos.) You can either register manually or use a service like Add Me (www.addme.com), which charges a small fee to register you on 1,500 worldwide search engines.

Bright Idea

When writing copy for your web site, keep it brief enough so each topic will fit on one screen, since many people find it annoying to have to keep scrolling down as they read.

organizations all across the country could use to solicit contributions for their causes. The cards were meant to be used to invite potential donors to an imaginary New Year's Eve dinner party. But instead of attending yet another boring rubber chicken affair, the donor had the luxury of making a contribution and staying home instead. The key to the campaign's success was the way humor was used throughout the card and the reply card the donors used when they sent in their checks.

Riddle hired a web page designer who took his rough drawings and instructions and turned them into an award-winning web site. The pages were colorful, interesting, and filled with free fundraising advice people could use by just visiting the site. Each fundraising plan came complete with sample cards, instructions, and a toll-free number to call.

Convinced he was the king of customer service, Riddle registered the web site with the appropriate search engines and waited for the money to start rolling in. But although the site received several hundred hits per day from visitors all across the United States and even a half-dozen foreign countries, no one placed an order.

"I had forgotten the most important rule when it comes to marketing via the internet: Your target audience had to be both online and internet-savvy," Riddle says. "But in this case, my target audience for the 'No Go, No Show' fundraising plan was small and midsized social service nonprofit organizations, most of which barely had computers, let alone internet access. Eventually, I realized this and pulled the web site."

The moral of the story, says Riddle: "Before you spend time and money putting together a web site for your consulting business, make sure the people you are trying to reach will be on the other end of the keyboard!"

Despite this caveat, however, there's no denying the internet is a powerful tool for businesses of all types. A recent Harris Interactive telephone survey determined that 73 percent of U.S. adults are now online, up from just 9 percent in 1995. So you'll want to at least consider harnessing the power of the internet for your consulting business in some way. You can't afford not to.

By Design

Here are some elements you might consider including on your own web page:

- *Flash intro.* This is a great tool for consultants who sell a "sexy" product or service (computer consultants and image consultants come to mind). Flash is an attention-getting tool that consists of moving images and/or audio sound bites meant to catch surfers' attention. If you decide to use flash, be sure to place a "skip intro" option on the flash page so eager (or impatient) readers can bypass your artwork and get to the point. For an example of an elaborate flash intro, check out the web site of Stantec, a professional design and consulting business, at www.stantec.com.

- *Service "menu"*. This page should describe in detail every service you offer. This is useful for two reasons: It gives surfers enough information to know whether they should contact you directly, and it allows you to suggest other services the customer might be interested in. Incidentally, it's not necessary to give prices on this page. It's almost always better to request that they call you to discuss their project before you divulge any financial details.

- *Portfolio*. As Schiavone mentioned, an online portfolio allows you to show actual samples of the work you've done. It's particularly useful for people who provide visual and communications arts services, but it also can be used by consultants in other fields whose completed projects can be photographed and downloaded to the site.

- *Biography*. If you have impressive credentials from previous corporate work or other projects, you might want to write a paragraph or two about your experience since it may convince prospects their work will be in good hands. Keep your own photograph off the site, however, unless your appearance has a direct bearing on the type of service you provide. For instance, it might be beneficial for a motivational speaker to include a photo, but there would be no need for an oil and gas industry consultant to show his or her face.

- *List of clients*. You might consider adding this later after you've gotten some successful jobs under your belt. If you can drop the names of a couple big-name clients, so much the better. Just be sure to ask each client's permission to use his or her name before publishing the information for all to see.

- *Contact information*. In addition to providing a phone and a fax number, it's a good idea to include an e-mail address for those who prefer making a cyber contact. Thanks to e-mail, you can do business with anyone anywhere in the world, so it's not necessary to divulge your location or mailing address on this page.

No matter what you decide to put on your site, make sure you update the information regularly so clients keep coming back. "I redo my web site completely about every two years to keep it fresh and current," says Huntington Beach, California, consultant Susan Bock. "My site is designed for and targeted to prospective clients, and keeping it current lends credibility to what I do."

Building Your Site

Unless you're putting up one of the free basic web sites available online or from your ISP, which come with easy-to-follow tutorials, you might want to leave the job of creating a web site to an experienced web page developer. In addition to understanding the

Site Seeing

The internet is not only a great place to get your name in front of potential clients—it's chock full of resources to help you in your business as well. The array of information can be overwhelming, but here are a few web sites to get you started:

○ *AARP (www.aarp.org):* provides information and resources for people age 50+

○ *Amazon (www.amazon.com):* huge online seller of books, CDs, DVDs, and more

○ *CPA Finder (www.cpafinder.com):* a listing of accountants by state

○ *eBay (www.ebay.com):* an amazing resource for buying or selling just about anything, from office equipment to office supplies

○ *Entrepreneur (www.entrepreneur.com):* the premier source for small-business advice

○ *FindLaw (www.findlaw.com):* a legal source with free information, tools, and resources, as well as an attorney finder

○ *Health Insurance In-Depth (www.healthinsuranceindepth.com):* a source for information about insurance basics and free health insurance quotes

○ *IRS (www.irs.ustreas.gov):* the official source for tax tips, advice, and publications. Also helpful is www.irs.gov/smallbiz, which has a wealth of info for small-business owners

○ *National Association for the Self-Employed (www.nase.org):* offers advice, group insurance, and more

○ *National Association of Women Business Owners (www.nawbo.org):* acts as the voice of 10.6 million women-owned businesses and offers business resources and tools

○ *National Small Business Network (www.businessknowhow.net):* a great source for free information and links to free trade publications

○ *SBA (www.sbaonline.sba.gov):* an invaluable resource for starting a small business

○ *U.S. Census Bureau (www.census.gov):* the government site for demographic and other population information

○ *USPS ZIP code lookup (http://zip4.usps.com/zip4/welcome.jsp):* a useful resource for direct-mail efforts

○ *Verizon's area code lookup (www22.verizon.com/areacodes):* look up by state or area code (so you know which state you're calling)

Stat Fact

Of the 73 percent of American adults now online, according to a recent Harris Interactive poll, 30 percent are college graduates and 48 percent have household incomes above $50,000. The heaviest users are adults aged 18 to 39, who make up 49 percent of the cyber population.

basics of HTML, the language of web sites, and all the technical aspects involved in building a site, they can advise you on technicalities like how information should be packaged for maximum impact and where links should be inserted to lead viewers from one screen to the next. They also can set the site up so you can update it yourself or add new content easily.

The cost of a professionally designed, fully functional web site with links is based on the number of pages on the site and typically will range from $1,000 to $4,000. It's customary for web designers to charge by the hour for future maintenance and/or updates on the site, which is a good reason to ask your designer to create a site that you can update yourself. To find a web designer, check the Yellow Pages, or contact your local chamber of commerce or other business organization.

If you're short on cash and you have the time and patience to take on the job yourself, you could try creating your own web page. There are a number of web page programs on the market, like Dreamweaver MX by Macromedia (retails for $399, www.macro media.com) or Microsoft FrontPage (retails for $199 or less, available from computer superstores), that can make the job easy for anyone who's at least somewhat computer savvy.

Once your web site is operational, you'll have to select an internet host site, which is the place in cyberspace where your site will reside. Examples of well-known internet hosts include EarthLink and NetPass, but there are many others to choose from. The main criteria to consider when choosing a host are how often the site goes down, how quickly it goes back online after experiencing downtime, and how long it has been in business. It's always best to choose a host that's well-established so you can be fairly confident it will be there to serve you in both the near and distant future.

You can expect to pay your web host about $19.95 per month for 20MB disk space. Some of the hosts also will allow you to register your domain name (discussed next) when you sign up, which saves you a step. But since web hosting is very competitive, it pays to shop around for the best deal. You can start with the host names you'll find in the Appendix at the end of this book.

Bright Idea

If you'd like to use your own name as your domain name, check out www.namesecure.com. For as low as $7.49 a year, you can register your name using one of the common commercial suffixes (.com, .net, .org, .biz or .info), and you'll receive services like unlimited web and e-mail forwarding.

Naming Rights

Before you can sign up with a web host, you must select and register a unique name, known as a domain name (or URL, for Universal Resource Locator). As with your business name, you'll want to use a name that best describes your business, as in www.david jonesassociates.com. With a common name like David Jones, however, it's possible someone else is already using the name. The company that registers your name will check it against other registered names before giving you the go ahead to use the one you've selected. For this reason, it's a good idea to have more than one name in mind when you're ready to register.

Domain names are registered for a minimum of two years at a cost of approximately $70. There are several companies that can register your name, but one of the best known is DOMAIN.com, which also offers five- and ten-year registrations at a cost of $23 and $18 per year, respectively.

Money
Matters

Now that we've explored the various elements that go into establishing your new consulting business, let's take a look at how you'll pay for them. In this chapter, you'll find out how to create a simple income and operating expense statement so you'll know how much money you need to make ends meet, then learn where you can get the cash you may need to finance your new venture. We'll also cover setting fees and how to get those checks rolling in.

Income and Operating Expenses

Keeping track of both income and operating expenses is crucial to the success of your business. Without a tool to track how much money you have coming in vs. the amount flowing out, you can quickly find yourself in financial trouble—trouble that can lead to the dissolution of your business.

Protect yourself by keeping track of all income and expenditures on a monthly basis. All you need is a simple income and operating expense (I&E) statement, which you can create easily using QuickBooks or a simple spreadsheet program like Excel. We've given you two sample I&E statements on pages 98 and 99 that show the operating expenses for two hypothetical consulting businesses. The first business, Retail Management Consulting, is a sole proprietorship, and David Jones and Associates is an S corporation with one full-time employee (the owner) and one administrative assistant. We've estimated monthly costs for each business to give you an idea of how much a new business might be expected to spend. Read on for details on what these costs entail, then plug in your own numbers on the worksheet on page 100.

Phone Charges

Phone rates vary widely across the country, but it's reasonable to estimate a cost of $33 per line. Extra features include voice mail, a must at about $12 to $18 per month, call waiting for approximately $5 per month, and caller ID for about $7.50 for number identification and $2 extra for name display. Caller ID is especially useful if you're using your home phone as your business line. A better deal may be a bundled package that includes these services as well as long-distance minutes. If you add an extra line for your fax machine or modem, you may be able to get a multiline discount, so shop around for the best price. For the purpose of this exercise, we are using $90 to represent the cost of two phone lines with voice mail.

If you carry a cellular phone (and who doesn't), and the phone is used strictly for business, the cost can go on your I&E, too. As mentioned in

Beware!

The IRS requires written records for any business expenses you deduct, including the cost of phone service or long-distance calls. Because it can be difficult to remember which phone numbers belong to which client on your itemized bill, keep a log of business calls that lists the date of the call, the company/individual name and the phone number.

Chapter 6, basic packages start at about $19.95 for hundreds of minutes of airtime, and go up to as much as $69.95 for plans with multiple phones and 400 or more minutes.

Postage

As mentioned in Chapter 10, you'll probably want to send out direct mail a couple of times a year to entice new prospects to use your consulting services. First-class postage is currently 37 cents, which is the best way to mail materials you actually want someone to open and read, vs. bulk mail, which often is perceived as junk mail. Because you'll probably be mailing out a lot of quotes, contracts, and reports, you should estimate extra postage costs to cover those as well.

Licenses

Unless you're doing work that requires you to have special licensing or certification (say, a hazardous waste control consultant), it's quite likely the only licensing you'll need will be a standard business license. This type of license is issued by the municipality in which you're based, and the cost varies. For simplicity's sake, we've used $30 on our sample I&E.

Salaries

If you're a one-man-band (no sexism intended), it's easy to figure out what to put on your I&E—just estimate how much you'd like to earn in a year and divide that amount by 12 to get a monthly figure. Just as an FYI, a recent survey by the Association of Management Consulting Firms reported that the average compensation for an entry-level consultant in a consulting practice was $61,496 (which included salary plus bonus or profit sharing). Although as a self-employed consultant you don't exactly fit that mold, the *Occupational Outlook Handbook 2004–05 Edition* says that self-employed consultants can make considerably more than that. For the sake of our hypothetical I&E, we've used an owner's salary of $3,350 per month, or just over $40,000 per year.

Entry-level and clerical employees often start at the federal minimum wage, which currently is $5.15. Some states (including Alaska, California, Connecticut, Delaware, Hawaii, Illinois, Kansas, Maine, Massachusetts, Ohio, Oregon, Rhode Island, Vermont, Washington, and the District of Columbia) have their own minimum wage laws, so you should check with your state's department

> **Smart Tip** Tip...
>
> It's usually a wise idea to live below your means during the start-up phase of your consulting business. While you'll have to cover your everyday living expenses, you may find that making a few financial sacrifices now could benefit the business tremendously later.

Sample Operating Income and Expenses

Retail Management Consulting

Projected Gross Monthly Income		$5,500
Projected Monthly Expenses		
Mortgage/rent	$0	
Phone (office and cell)	130	
Utilities (water only)	0	
Postage	25	
Licenses	30	
Owner salary	3,35	
Employee wages	0	
Benefits/taxes	335	
Advertising/promotion	100	
Legal services	20	
Accounting services	100	
Office supplies	64	
Insurance	125	
Transportation	10	
Subscriptions/dues	30	
Loan repayment	0	
Online service	20	
Web hosting	20	
Miscellaneous	444	
Total Projected Monthly Expenses	$4,893	
Projected Net Monthly Income		$607

Sample Operating Income and Expenses

David Jones and Associates

Projected Gross Monthly Income		$8,000
Projected Monthly Expenses		
Mortgage/rent	$0	
Phone (office and cell)	130	
Utilities (water only)	0	
Postage	25	
Licenses	30	
Owner salary	3,350	
Employee wages	412	
Benefits/taxes	380	
Advertising/promotion	200	
Legal services	75	
Accounting services	100	
Office supplies	70	
Insurance	225	
Transportation	100	
Subscriptions/dues	125	
Loan repayment	0	
Online service	40	
Web hosting	20	
Miscellaneous	528	
Total Projected Monthly Expenses	$5,810	
Projected Net Monthly Income		$2,190

▲

Operating Income and Expenses Worksheet

Projected Gross Monthly Income $ _____

Projected Monthly Expenses

Mortgage/rent   _____

Phone (office and cell)   _____

Utilities (water only)   _____

Postage   _____

Licenses   _____

Owner salary   _____

Employee wages   _____

Benefits/taxes   _____

Advertising/promotion   _____

Legal services   _____

Accounting services   _____

Office supplies   _____

Insurance   _____

Transportation   _____

Subscriptions/dues   _____

Loan repayment   _____

Online service   _____

Web hosting   _____

Miscellaneous   _____

Total Projected Monthly Expenses $ _____

Projected Net Monthly Income $ _____

of labor for the current wage. On our I&E we figured in a wage for a 20-hour-a-week aide at $5.15 an hour (or $103 per week).

A more skilled employee such as a consulting associate would of course be paid at a higher rate, possibly as high as $20 per hour. Ask your association colleagues how much they pay to see what the market will bear.

Benefits and Taxes

As you'll recall from Chapter 7, offering benefits can be a good way to retain good help. But the fact is, many small-business owners can't afford to offer much more than perhaps a one-week paid vacation or the occasional sick day. So although benefits do make people happy, it's not always possible to offer them. But if you do decide to offer benefits like medical insurance, you can assume that your cost will be 8 to 10 percent of the employee's hourly income.

But one thing that's not negotiable is payroll taxes. As you know from Chapter 7, there's a whole slew of taxes you'll have to pay on employees' wages, including the FICA tax, Federal Unemployment Tax, state unemployment tax, and workers' compensation insurance. Since you don't have previous records to compare to, you should estimate high so you're not caught short. Your accountant can help you make a reasonable guess.

Incidentally, if you're using subcontractors (aka independent contractors), they are fully responsible for their own taxes. Just make sure you comply with the IRS' definition of independent contractors. (As we mentioned in Chapter 7, IRS Publication 15-A, *Employer's Supplemental Tax Guide*, can give you more information about the employee/independent contractor distinction.) "I use subcontractors precisely because I don't want to be bothered with tax issues," says Merrily Schiavone in Newark, Delaware.

Then there are the taxes you'll pay as a sole proprietor on your own earnings, beginning with estimated taxes. The IRS requires you to make quarterly estimated tax payments on your income, and in fact will charge you a hefty penalty if you don't pay enough in the quarter in which the taxes are due. But as you can imagine, estimating taxes when you're starting a new business can be tricky. Consult with your accountant for help, or if you want to simplify matters, take your projected income, multiply it by 40 percent, and send that amount in, divided appropriately between Uncle Sam and your state's treasury department. (You can find out what your state's current tax rate is by contacting the treasury department.) If that sounds really high, you're right—it is. And one

Smart Tip

It's not always necessary to wait until you have a lot of capital to start your business. For many consultants, the only initial overhead will be business cards, a brochure, and postage to get the information to potential clients. But someone like a computer consultant will need to invest in a wide variety of equipment. In that case, you'd need a start-up loan.

reason why it's so high is because the federal government assesses a self-employment tax on entrepreneurs, which is the other half of the Social Security and Medicare taxes. (Remember, you're the employer of record, so you have to foot the entire bill.)

If you form an S corporation, you're also required to pay estimated taxes on any money you earn, even if all the money stays in the corporation. As the result of the Jobs and Growth Tax Relief Reconciliation Act of 2003, the top corporate tax rate for an S corporation is 35 percent, down from 38.6 percent. You could pay less, depending on the amount you earn and the number of deductions you're eligible for.

It should be pretty apparent that tax issues can be very complex. We strongly recommend that you consult your accountant to make sure you're paying enough taxes and paying them on time.

What will an accountant cost? It's safe to estimate that you'll use an accountant no more than five hours a month. The Occupational Outlook says that accountants' median salaries were $47,000 in a recent year, which works out to $22.60 an hour. We've rounded that figure down to $20 an hour and plugged $100 per month into our sample I&E.

Office Supplies

You'll need a variety of supplies every month, including pens, legal pads, report covers, computer paper, and other supplies. For other expenses like business printing that aren't incurred every month, add up the figures you arrived at for your start-up expenses worksheet in Chapter 6 and divide them by 12 to get a estimated figure for your I&E.

Advertising

These expenses can add up, so you'll want to estimate them as closely as possible. Don't forget to include the cost of producing direct-mail pieces, newspaper advertising, and any other business awareness efforts you may decide to do, as well as your Yellow Pages advertising costs. You should also include your publicity costs (like for news releases) here just to make things simple.

Insurance

If you did the insurance exercise in Chapter 5, you already have a pretty good idea of how much business and personal insurance you'll need. Tally the cost of the annual premiums, divide that by 12, and plug that number into your I&E.

Transportation

As a consultant, you're likely to be on the road a lot. So this is the place to figure in the cost to run and maintain your vehicle, including gasoline, tune-ups, windshield wiper fluid, oil changes, and other motoring costs like tolls. If you're consulting in an urban area that has a reliable transportation network, like New York City or Seattle, you'll want

> **Beware!**
> The IRS won't object if your family vehicle doubles as business transportation as long as you keep careful written records on the number of miles you drive for each purpose. You're allowed to deduct only the percentage of the insurance costs, the loan payment, maintenance, gasoline, etc., that pertains to the business.

to include your subway, bus, or other transportation costs on this line instead. For the purposes of our sample I&E statement, we've estimated $100 per month to represent the cost of driving for business.

Magazine Subscriptions

As discussed in Chapter 8, magazines and trade publications are a good way to stay current on issues of importance to you and your clients, so you'll probably want to subscribe to a number of different general and specialty consulting publications. Include their cost on your operating statement.

Membership Dues

Among the types of membership dues you'll want to include here are the costs to join industry-specific organizations and local business organizations like the chamber of commerce. Refer back to Chapter 8 for a list of the major organizations that service consultants.

Loan Repayment

If you purchased a vehicle for use in your business, the loan payment figure goes on your monthly expense report. This is also where you'd include repayment of any loans from family, friends, and investors, if applicable.

Internet Service Fees

Internet connection fees vary widely. Here's a recap of the approximate amounts you can expect to pay:

- Standard ISP: $20 to $25 per month
- ISDN: $50 a month, plus $20 to $25 a month for an ISP connection
- DSL: $30 to $40 a month
- Cable modem: $40 a month, plus basic cable TV service at the very least
- Broadband high-speed satellite internet: $99 a month

Other Miscellaneous Expenses

It's always a good idea to add 10 percent of the bottom line total to cover miscellaneous expenses, some of which won't crop up until you've actually started consulting.

Financing Your Start-Up

One of the great things about being a consultant is that you really don't need much cash to launch your business. For instance, Costa Mesa, California, consultant David McMullen started his computer business for just a few hundred dollars, which was all he needed to buy a few office supplies, business cards, a computer repair kit, and a new briefcase. For this reason, many consultants use personal savings or plastic to buy a new computer and the other supplies needed to open for business. But let's say you're thinking big and you need more cash to buy a building or purchase a specialty piece of equipment. Then you'll undoubtedly need to obtain financing to make your dreams a reality.

Because as a new business owner you won't have a track record of success yet, your best bet is to approach small financial institutions like community banks. You also may find that credit unions will be more willing to work with you.

Other sources of financing include:

- *SBA.* This government agency offers a number of different loan programs as well as free counseling and training.

- *Unsecured personal loan.* This type of loan is usually much easier to obtain than a business loan. Important note: Good credit is a must to qualify.

- *Personal capital.* Sometimes it pays to tap into your own resources rather than to ask someone else for a buck, since it saves on finance charges and preserves your peace of mind. In fact, funding a start-up out of personal savings, as both Merrily Schiavone and Huntington Beach, California, consultant Susan Bock did, is often the preferred choice for many aspiring consultants because the amount required to launch the business is so low.

"One good thing about paying out of personal savings is that you can stay solvent when business is off because you don't have loans to pay back," Schiavone says. "The business climate has been treacherous for me since 9/11 because most of my customers cut back on marketing. I also had a couple of big contracts end when the person I was dealing with left the company. Having no overhead and no loans to repay meant I could make it through the bad times."

"Just be sure to have sufficient funds to sustain the business for several months," Bock adds. "The ability to sustain yourself is a crucial element in your success

Smart Tip

Tip...

Because it can be difficult for an aspiring entrepreneur to obtain a large start-up loan, it may be wise to start your consulting business as a side job while you're still employed full time. This allows you to both set aside money for the start-up and establish a record of success that will impress your banker.

because business can be very cyclical, and since often no two years are the same, it can be hard to predict your income stream."

- *Home equity line of credit (HELOC) loan.* Your bank may not be willing to give you a HELOC for a business start-up, but it's worth asking.
- *Credit cards.* This is a popular choice for many entrepreneurs. Just spend wisely. You don't want to start your new career with a huge amount of debt hanging over your head.
- *Family and friends.* To avoid losing a friend or breaking up a family over money squabbles, handle the transaction in a professional, businesslike way.

Smart Tip

Tip...

It pays to establish a relationship with a local banker even if you don't need start-up capital. You never know when you might need a short-term loan to complete a project that has many upfront costs (such as interior design work or the purchase of expensive new equipment) that might not be fully covered by the advance you requested.

How Much Should You Charge?

Have you heard the one about the newspaper printing plant that is in serious trouble because its presses stopped running due to a mechanical malfunction? Unless the presses start again within the next few hours, the newspaper won't be on the newsstands when the sun comes up. The repair people on the job are stumped and cannot figure out why the presses have stopped working. So they call in a consultant, not worrying about the high fee they no doubt know they'll be charged because of the late hour. But it doesn't matter, because the first priority is to get those presses running again.

The consultant comes in, takes a few minutes to examine the printing presses and goes over to one of the gears and taps it with a wrench. Within seconds, the presses resume rolling, and the papers make it to the newsstands in the nick of time.

When the consultant submits his bill for $1,005, he is asked why he is charging such an odd amount. "Simple," he replies. "The $5 is for tapping the gear and $1,000 is for knowing which gear to tap!"

So when you set your fees, remember that people are willing to pay you for knowing which gear to tap!

If you charge too little, you won't succeed in business. If you charge too much, you won't get any clients. So how do you find that middle ground that seems fair to everyone involved? One way to help you decide how much to charge is to find out what the competition's rates are. A simple telephone call to ask for their brochure and rates

Bill Me

Consultants often find themselves puzzled about how to set fees. They feel guilty if they set them too high, but they also know they may not be able to stay in business if they set them too low.

So to survive as a consultant in any industry, you need to have fees that will enable you to stay in business; at the same time, both you and your clients need to feel that your fees are fair and equitable. Always remember that as long as you provide a service to a client who is willing to pay for your services and your fees are reasonable (and comparable to others in the industry), you have reached the so-called "middle ground" when it comes to fee structures. For help setting your fees, contact the membership organization that services the industry in which you work and ask what their research shows. Then sit back, relax and enjoy cashing those checks.

should do the trick. Then set your rates so you are competitive with everyone else in the community.

Before setting your fees, make sure you have listed all your expenses. There is nothing worse than setting your rates, having your client pay you on time and then finding out you failed to include several expenses that materialized. This brings up an important point to remember in every job you take from a client: Include a "miscellaneous" line item in your fee proposal. But don't pad the miscellaneous figure to make additional income.

Keep one important rule in mind when establishing your fee, no matter which structure you decide on: The more money people pay for a product or service, the more they expect to get for their money. In other words, if a client agrees to your hourly rate of $400, then you had better give $400 worth of service every hour you work for that client.

When setting your rates, you have several options, including hourly rates, project fees, and working on a retainer basis. Let's examine each one closely.

Hourly Fees

You need to tread carefully when setting hourly fees, because two things could happen:

1. Your hourly rate is so high that no one could ever afford you (therefore no client will ever knock on your door).

2. Your hourly rate is so low that no one will take you seriously.

Some clients prefer to be billed on an hourly basis, while others hate the idea of paying someone what they perceive to be too much per hour. Such clients usually prefer to pay per project, which we'll discuss shortly.

Fundraising consultant John Riddle in Bear, Delaware, has had many clients ask to be billed on an hourly basis. Since all those clients were nonprofit organizations, it became clear that because a board of directors was ultimately

Beware!
Don't set your fees too high; you may pick up a few clients in the beginning, but unless your rates are competitive—and fair—you will fail miserably as a consultant.

responsible for the financial health of those agencies, they were more comfortable working with a fundraising consultant who charged by the hour. It makes it easier for some nonprofits to determine their actual fundraising costs when an hourly billing system is used. Most fundraising consultants charge between $150 and $300 per hour, depending on the demographics of the community.

Project Rates

When working on a project rate basis, a consultant normally gets a fixed amount of money for a predetermined period of time. A few of Riddle's fundraising clients preferred to be charged this way, so it wasn't unusual for him to charge $36,000 for a one-year project in which he consulted with them on how they could raise money. Because of the amount of money involved, most agencies preferred to be billed on a monthly basis.

This worked out fine until Riddle realized that many agencies were late paying their monthly bills. Because of this, he decided that all future clients who wished to be billed on a monthly basis would pay the first month's fee and the last month's fee at the signing of the contract, which meant that if the agreed-upon amount of the project was $36,000, to be paid on a monthly basis, he received a check in the amount of $6,000 before beginning any work ($3,000 for the first month's fee and $3,000 for the last month's fee).

Dollar Stretcher
When you print your brochure or other information about your consulting business, don't include your rates. Instead, print your prices on a special insert. That way, you can change rates without having to reprint the entire brochure.

Retainer Basis

Working on a retainer basis gives you a set monthly fee in which you agree to be available for work for an agreed-upon number of hours for your client. While in the ideal world you would have a dozen or so clients who hire you and pay you a hefty sum each month (and never actually call you except for a few hours here and there), don't get your hopes up. Most companies that hire a consultant on a retainer basis have a clause in their contract that prohibits you from working for their competitors.

Working and getting paid by this method certainly has its advantages. You are guaranteed income each month, and when you are starting out in your consulting business, cash flow can be a problem. Some consultants actually offer a percentage reduction in their fees if a client will agree to pay a monthly retainer fee. The average income when a consultant is paid on a retainer basis is $3,500 per month.

Bonus Options

It is not unusual for consultants to have some type of bonus option in their letter of agreement or contract with their clients. A bonus may be a percentage of an amount that the consultant saves a client (if the consultant has been hired to reorganize a department or division, for example), or in the case of Riddle's fundraising clients, a percentage of the amount he raised for them.

Sometime ago, he had a client who asked if he would work as a fundraising consultant getting paid only a percentage of any money he raised for the organization. He counteroffered with a small monthly retainer fee and reduced the percentage rate they originally offered. This way, he would receive something each month for the work he would be doing, and he was still guaranteed a bonus.

He ended up charging the client $2,000 per month for 12 months and was to receive 10 percent of any foundation or corporate grants he was successful in obtaining. So at the end of the first year, he had been paid $24,000 in retainer fees and received a bonus in the amount of $17,000 (which was 10 percent of the $170,000 raised). The client had originally offered him 20 percent (which would have given him only $34,000); so in this case, he ended up earning more with a lower percent rate and a fixed monthly retainer rate (the client paid him $41,000 total, $7,000 more than he would have made if he had opted for the straight 20 percent). It doesn't always work out that way, but again, depending on your cash flow situation, it may work in your favor to have a bonus option. The average bonus is 15 to 20 percent of the funds obtained for the organization.

Billings and Collections

It's easy to get into a cash-flow crunch very quickly if you don't bill on a regular basis. One way to make sure money is always coming in from your clients is to build a payment schedule into your contract. Typically, consultants request a partial payment on the first of the month for the duration of the contract if they're on retainer; or half upfront and half at the end of the contract if they work on a per-project or hourly rate. Others, like Schiavone, prefer to wait until the work is completely finished before asking for payment. "I prefer to be sure that my customer is completely satisfied before I send a bill," she says.

Checks in the Mail

Here are five ways to keep the checks coming in while you are between jobs:

1. *Write articles for your local newspaper.* Virtually every newspaper in the United States buys material from local freelance writers. And since you are a professional in your chosen field, you should have no difficulty writing articles for those newspapers. Such articles enhance your portfolio and are bound to impress potential clients.

2. *Write articles for trade journals relative to your niche.* For instance, if you are a marketing consultant, send articles to marketing journals and magazines. Consider the publications to which you already subscribe as good candidates for your material. But don't stop at that list; check out *Writer's Market* (Writer's Digest Books) and the *Literary Market Place* (Information Today) in your local library.

3. *Work for a temporary employment agency.* Depending how much time you have available, you may work for a few days or a few weeks just to keep money coming in. But if you choose this route, don't forget to keep marketing your services.

4. *Teach a course at your local college.* Check with your local college's employment office to see if there are any openings for an instructor for the non-credit courses offered. If there are no openings for instructors, consider offering a new course. Another option for teaching a workshop is to offer one free of charge. You may not get paid, but you will get free publicity for your business.

5. *Write a book.* Did you know that it is possible to sell a book idea on the basis of just an outline and a sample chapter? Writer's Digest Books (www.writers digest.com/store/books) has several excellent tomes that explain how to get published. By writing and having a book published about the industry in which you have chosen to consult, you will add credibility to your work as a consultant.

> ⚠️ **Beware!**
>
> Pay quarterly taxes on your earnings, including bonuses. Otherwise you could be in for a real shock (as in an underpayment penalty) if you wait until April 15 to pay tax on any substantial earnings you receive from your clients.

When it comes to getting those bills out, Bock recommends sending invoices electronically rather than on paper, since it gets them into the hands of the client faster. QuickBooks has an invoicing function to make creating those invoices easier.

What happens when the check's not in the mail? Collections are an unavoidable part of doing business. It's not uncommon for companies and individuals to ignore your stated terms, or to stretch them out as long as possible before paying. Still others won't pay until after you've started collection proceedings like sending reminder bills and placing collection calls.

To avoid collection problems, it really is a good idea to ask for one-half of your fee upfront, particularly when you're dealing with a new client. You also should include clearly stated payment terms in your contract, like specifying that full payment is due upon delivery of the agreed-upon work.

Today's accounting software packages, including QuickBooks, include collection management tools to streamline the collection process. In fact, QuickBooks by Intuit is a good choice for all your accounting needs. The Pro version for Windows retails for $299.95, and you can use it to generate invoices, track receivables, write checks, pay bills, and more. It's particularly useful because it interfaces seamlessly with Microsoft Word, Excel, and TurboTax. You can find QuickBooks at office supply and computer stores. Another popular accounting package is Peachtree Accounting from Best Software SB, which retails for $199.95. It's available from computer stores or directly from Peachtree (www.peachtree.com).

Should You Accept Credit Cards?

As you can tell from the examples in this chapter, consultants can command a large fee for their expertise. For this reason, you may wish to consider accepting credit cards for the services you provide. It can be an especially good idea to provide this payment method if you offer workshops or seminars, or if you sell subscriptions to a newsletter. Research has proved that people will not hesitate to plunk

> **Smart Tip** *Tip...*
>
> When accepting credit cards, think beyond MasterCard and Visa. Many of your clients will prefer to use American Express and possibly the Discover card. Check with your bank to see what credit-card options you have for your consulting business.

down their charge card to buy something at a seminar or trade show. But those same people will more often than not hesitate to write a check for that product or service.

Shop around with local banks to see which can offer you the best rate. Rates generally depend on such factors as monthly sales volume and whether you have been a commercial customer for some time.

Depending on who your client base is, your regular consulting clients will probably not pay using their credit cards, yet it is still a good idea to offer this payment method. Accepting credit cards could put the odds in your favor when a potential client is deciding between you or your competitor's company.

Avoiding Cash-Flow Problems

So far we've discussed your potential for making money. But it bears mentioning that many consulting businesses fail simply because they experience too many cash-flow problems. Cash-flow problems affect both large and small businesses every day in this country, so don't feel bad if you run into some temporary cash-flow problems. Here are some ways to avoid the cash-flow blues:

- Before you sign any contract or letter of agreement, make sure you have double- and triple-checked the budget you have proposed. Go over each line item and expense carefully, because the time to spot trouble is before it begins.
- Consider asking for the first and last month's fees upfront (at the signing of the contract), or at least ask for one-third of the amount you expect to collect. This, of course, will depend on who your client is, how healthy his or her organization's cash-flow situation is, and so on.

If your clients have failed to keep up their end of the payment schedule, refuse to continue working until payments have been brought up to date. Make sure you have a clause in your contract or letter of agreement addressing this problem; otherwise, a client may have you over a legal barrel.

Writing Winning
Contracts and
Reports

To be an effective consultant, you must learn how to get your message across to your clients. When you find the ideal solutions to their problems, you want to be able to present them in a written format that is easy to understand. This means, then, that you need to be a good communicator to be a good consultant, and the way you'll express yourself

▲

will be in solid, winning reports that spell out in detail your findings and recommendations.

But before you can get to the point where you can wrap up a job and report back to the client, you've got to land the work. That means coming to terms with the client before undertaking a project, and the easiest way to do that is by writing a formal contract. In addition to spelling out all the terms of your agreement, a contract can help you avoid what Susan Bock, a Huntington Beach, California, consultant, calls "project creep," in which you begin with a specific task that morphs into more work than you agreed to as the project proceeds. Having a signed contract that details exactly what you've agreed to do will help you rein in projects before they take on a life of their own.

In this chapter, you'll find tips for writing effective contracts as well as sample reports you can use as inspiration when you're ready to create your own.

Contract Pointers

Often new consultants don't see the need for formal contracts, especially if they remember "the good old days" when people did business on an oral agreement or a handshake. Back then, when people gave you their word, you knew they would honor their end of the bargain. But times have changed. No longer can business be conducted without something in writing. You need a written document to protect both parties in any type of business arrangement.

A detailed contract or letter of agreement will alleviate any misunderstandings in any type of consulting agreement and should be carefully reviewed by both parties before anyone signs on the bottom line. It doesn't matter who you are working for, either. In fact, if you are consulting for someone you know, be extra careful and make sure everything that is expected of you is put into writing. When money is involved, friendships can go sour very quickly.

What is a contract? In simple terms, a contract is an agreement between two parties in which one party agrees to do something in return for something of value. Contracts can be very simple one-page documents, or they can be 100 pages long or more, depending on the subject matter and how many complicated issues they cover indepth. Some smaller nonprofit organizations prefer signing a letter of agreement over a contract because it seems less formal than a contract; keep in mind, though, that a letter of agreement is still a binding agreement, enforceable by law. For a sample letter of agreement and contract for a fundraising consultant, see pages 120 and 121.

> **Tip...**
>
> **Smart Tip**
>
> Let your contract or letter of agreement sit for 24 hours before you sign on the dotted line. Sometimes a good night's sleep will bring details into a whole new light.

Beware!
Listen to your intuition. If something doesn't feel right about what a client wants or expects, make sure every point is clarified in your contract or letter of agreement. Leave nothing to chance.

Wish List

When negotiating a consulting contract, keep these four elements always in mind:

1. What must the consultant have to get the job done?
2. What would the consultant like to have to get the job done?
3. What must the client have accomplished?
4. What would the client like to have accomplished?

When Bear, Delaware, consultant John Riddle considers taking on a fundraising client, he has certain expectations before he even gets to the first meeting. For example, he knows that if the organization wants him to develop a fundraising plan and show them how to raise money from foundations, corporations, small businesses, and/or individual contributors, he needs access to certain financial records. He usually asks for budgets, audits, long-range planning reports, and lists of all sources of income for the past five years.

The next thing you'll have to figure out is your minimum monetary requirement for a given project. Once you have set your fees, you should be able to communicate to your client the amount of money you need to get the job done. The first rule in the consulting business is to be flexible. (But don't sell yourself short; get paid what you are worth.) So when you decide on a figure, make sure it includes the dollar amount you must have to get the job done in a reasonable amount of time. (When it comes to quoting a figure, leave room for some negotiation; some clients prefer to have you reduce your rates by a few dollars or percentage points. It gives them a feeling of satisfaction.)

Obviously, every consultant would love to have every client pay the highest possible fees. But you must be reasonable when it comes to money matters; after all, both you and your client are in business. And to stay in business, you cannot let your fee structure rule.

In addition to those items, Riddle would like to have the cooperation of everyone on the board of directors, as well as be able to interview some of the organization's past donors, even though he knows he can still get results without these additional requirements.

Meeting Your Client's Needs

When a client hires you to perform consulting services, that client will also have certain expectations that must be fulfilled. It is your responsibility to see to it that all your client's needs are met. They must feel as if they are not only getting their money's worth,

What's in a Contract?

Every contract has three key elements, and all three elements must be present for the contract to be valid.

1. *Each contract must contain an offer.* An offer is simply something that is proposed by a person or business. For example, some of John Riddle's fundraising clients prefer a contract over a letter of agreement, so the offer may read something like this: "... will act on behalf of the XYZ nonprofit organization as a fundraising consultant to raise the necessary funds required. ..."

2. *Each contract must contain acceptance.* Acceptance is when one party accepts the terms offered in the contract. It is usually a good idea to put a time limit on any contract—or even a simple letter of agreement—you offer a client. For example, when Riddle presents a contract to new fundraising clients, he tells them that the offer will expire in a set number of days unless it is signed and accepted.

3. *Each contract must contain consideration.* This means payday! For example, the contract will read something like "... in exchange for a monthly payment of $5,000."

but they are also getting the job done on time (and under budget). In addition, most clients would like to have additional services performed—without cost to them, of course.

So when negotiating, keep in mind that the client secretly hopes that you will be able to provide them with some type of extra service. For example, almost all Riddle's fundraising clients hint that they would love to have additional information on potential funding sources but are usually reluctant to pay for additional research time. Because of this, he builds in some additional revenue when he quotes a fee for the services they contract for and is able to provide the additional data—at what appears to be "no additional charge."

The Fine Art of Negotiating

Here are a few tips not only to help boost your confidence when negotiating contracts, but also to help you leave a favorable impression on your client:

- *Smile and relax.* Take a deep breath and don't sweat the small stuff. Remember, if you look relaxed and happy, your client will be, too.

- *Make your first impression count.* How many times have you met people and, for whatever reason, decided you would rather have nothing to do with them?

Well, the same holds true in client-consultant relationships: First impressions count. So make yours an excellent one.

- *Go to the meeting prepared.* Your client will probably ask you some questions to test your knowledge of the subject in which you claim to be an expert. So make sure you are up-to-date on the latest information in your field.

Bright Idea

To give your important correspondence the weight it deserves, send documents to your clients via courier or overnight delivery service.

Setting the Tone

The first client-consultant meeting sets the tone for the entire relationship. Here are some important items to keep in mind when you go to that first meeting:

○ *What is your client's personality?* Does your client have an aggressive, take-charge management style? Or is the client more of a "let's get to know each other before we do business" type of person? The sooner you discover your client's personality, the easier it will be for you to get the job done.

○ *What is your client's problem?* Does your client know what the organization's problem is? Or are you being asked to find out what its problem is and come up with the solution? More often than not, a client will have a good idea about the problem and how to solve it. Make sure you agree with your client on what the real problem is before you agree to accept a contract.

○ *Is your client ready to accept your recommendations?* Make sure your client has an open mind and is willing to listen to your recommendations.

○ *Can you agree on a timetable?* Although most clients would like you to solve their problems in a few days, most are reasonable when it comes to giving you the time you need to solve those problems. However, you will sometimes run into clients who have a hard time understanding why you can't solve their problems overnight. Unless you can convince clients at the initial meeting that a reasonable timetable needs to be agreed upon, you might want to reconsider signing any contract with them.

○ *Can you outline who will take responsibility for each task?* Make certain that everything is spelled out in writing and that the contract clearly states who is responsible for each task.

- *Be ready to listen.* The true test of your listening skills will take place at the initial client meeting. This is where your clients will talk about what they really want and when they expect it to be accomplished.

- *Take plenty of notes.* Information will be flying right and left across the room. Take accurate notes, because your contract or letter of agreement probably will be based on the notes you take during the initial meeting.

> ### Smart Tip
> Write several drafts of your final report for your client. Determine which version will be the easiest to understand. Don't forget to keep your report simple, and use plenty of bulleted lists.

- *Be sure to ask plenty of questions.* Only then can you accurately determine what the client wants and expects. To find out what to ask, see the 20 Questions worksheet starting on page 123.

It's the Law

Once you have a signed contract and you've received that first partial payment, then you're home free, right? Not necessarily. The law says that either party can terminate a contract if any of the following has taken place:

- *Duress.* Neither party must use force or pressure—and that includes both the mental and physical kind—to get the contract signed.

- *Fraud.* If either party intentionally misrepresents himself or something he promises to deliver (or pay for), then fraud is present. And when fraud is present, the contract can be null and void.

- *Legality.* The contract you are about to sign must be for a transaction that is legal. For example, if a consultant put in a contract to fundraising clients that he or she would use any means necessary to raise the funds they need—including stealing, if the need presented itself—then the contract would be no good.

- *Capacity.* Each party who enters into the contract must be of legal age and sound mind, and not under the influence of alcohol or drugs. (Surely no consultant would sign a contract under these conditions, but who knows?)

- *Full disclosure.* If either party fails—on purpose—to disclose a key piece of information, the contract will be unenforceable.

Before we end this discussion of contracts, we have to acknowledge that there are consultants out there who don't work by contract. For instance, Merrily Schiavone in Newark, Delaware, operates on a handshake basis because she says Delaware is such a small state that everyone knows everyone else. But unless you're a very experienced consultant or you're working with clients you've had for years (like Schiavone), it's usually better to draw up a contract.

Sample Reports

Once you've completed a job to the client's satisfaction, it's time to report your findings. This serves two purposes. First, it demonstrates to your client exactly what you've done and how you've fulfilled the requirements of the contract. Second, it serves as a written record of your activities that can be used as an idea starter for future work. However, as we mentioned in a previous chapter, it's never a good idea to try to use a report written for one client as a boilerplate document for all the others that follow. After all, clients and their needs differ, and since they're paying the big bucks for your expertise and imagination, they deserve to have a report tailored to their situation.

Having said that, there's no reason why you can't look at other consultants' reports for inspiration, since having a firsthand look at how consultants present their solutions and how they format the documents can be very helpful when you write your own reports. For this reason, we've included a sample consulting report on page 125, which was prepared by John Riddle, the Bear, Delaware, consultant, for an actual client. Read through it to get an idea of one way to attack the report-writing process.

Smart Tip

Tip...

In your report, specify who is going to be responsible for each task; unless you specify in writing who is doing what, both you and your client may assume that the other person will be doing the work that is required.

As a consultant, you will also need to provide periodic updates to your client in writing. These help keep the lines of communication open and avoid any potential problems. Your update can be as simple and direct as the sample on page 128, once used by Riddle for a fundraising client.

Sample Letter of Agreement

1. In exchange for a one-time fee of $5,000 and 10 percent of any grants or contributions received from foundation or corporate sources, John Doe will submit grant requests, along with supporting documentation (which will be supplied by the organization) to 50 different funding sources.

2. John Doe will deliver the letters and grant proposals, ready for the organization's signature, no later than (insert date here). Postage costs will be the responsibility of the organization.

3. The organization will pay John Doe 10 percent of any foundation or corporate grant money that is received within 10 working days of receiving any checks. This 10 percent clause will remain in effect for one year and will expire on (insert date here).

4. John Doe warrants that he is qualified to research funding sources and write grant request letters and proposals. The organization understands that the appropriate foundations and corporations will make the funding decisions and that no promise is made as to how much money will be raised.

5. There is no limit on the amount of funding that the organization can ask for. However, based on research, John Doe will advise the organization as to the appropriate amount to solicit as a grant or corporate contribution.

6. The organization will pay John Doe a check in the amount of $5,000 on (insert date here). Within 10 days of receiving the check, John Doe will deliver the first batch of fundraising letters and grant proposals ready for the organization's signature. The remaining letters will be delivered no later than (insert date here).

This letter of agreement is in effect upon the signature of both parties.

The above terms are agreed to and accepted by:

_____   _____

(organization's representative signature and title)   (date)

_____   _____

(consultant's signature)   (date)

Sample Contract

This document outlines the agreement made on _____ (date) for services rendered by John Doe, hereinafter referred to as the CONSULTANT, and _____ (name of the person in the organization), as represented by _____ (name of the person signing the contract), hereinafter referred to as the ORGANIZATION.

1. Statement of Work: During the terms of this Agreement, the CONSULTANT will perform services as requested by the ORGANIZATION from _____ (date services will begin) and ending upon _____ (date services will terminate).

2. Travel Arrangements: (If your client is in your hometown and no travel is required, then omit this section.) The CONSULTANT will be arriving on _____ (date you will be arriving) and departing on _____ (date you will be leaving) and requests that the ORGANIZATION make hotel reservations that are billed directly to the ORGANIZATION for the night(s) of _____ (nights you will be staying in the hotel). Please secure late arrival and the ability to charge meals and telephone calls to the hotel room.

3. Payment: The ORGANIZATION shall pay the CONSULTANT according to the following schedule:

The fee of _____ (agreed-upon fee) made payable to the CONSULTANT as agreed upon in writing by both parties with additional expenses being paid by the ORGANIZATION. (If you fail to mention who is paying for additional expenses not covered by your fee, you run the risk of having to cover those expenses yourself.) The fee schedule is as follows: _____

_____

_____

(Outline in detail when you wish to receive payment; otherwise, some clients will send you a check whenever they feel like it. It's customary to specify that a payment is due on the first working day of the month and that if a payment has not been received within 10 days, the consultant reserves the right to temporarily halt any work until such payment has been made.)
(continued)

Sample Contract, continued

4. Relationship of Consultant: The CONSULTANT will serve as an independent contractor and will be responsible for all income taxes.

5. Interpretation of Agreement: This agreement may not be changed except in writing, signed by the CONSULTANT and an authorized official of the ORGANIZATION. This contract contains the specific terms of the agreement as governed by the laws of the state in which the ORGANIZATION is based.

6. Specific Needs: The CONSULTANT will provide _____

_____

(*specify the type of consulting services you will provide*) services to the ORGANIZATION.

7. Consultant Needs: The CONSULTANT will require the following documentation to complete the terms of the contract: _____

_____

(*Simply state what information you require from your client to get the job done; for example, you may need financial and historical records to develop a plan—this is where you would list those needs.*)

8. Cancellation Clause: Either the CONSULTANT or the ORGANIZATION may terminate this contract by serving notice in writing. A 10-day notice is required to cancel a contract before the term of the contract has expired. (*The number of days can be any number you and your client agree on; 10 days to two weeks is the norm in the industry.*)

In Witness Whereof, the Parties hereto have executed this Agreement as of _____ (*date you sign the contract*). Please return two signed copies of this Agreement to the CONSULTANT no later than five business days after receipt.

ORGANIZATION:

Name: _____ (signature)

Title: _____ Date: _____

CONSULTANT:

Name: _____ (signature)

Title: _____ Date: _____

20 Questions

What better way to learn what your clients want and expect (and how much they are willing to pay for your expertise) than to ask questions? Here are 20 questions you should ask a potential client before signing any contract or letter of agreement:

1. Can you define the problem you are experiencing?

   _____

   _____

2. How long has the problem affected your business?

   _____

   _____

3. Have you taken any steps on your own to solve the problem?

   _____

   _____

4. Why do you think the problem is occurring?

   _____

   _____

5. What are your overall objectives on this project?

   _____

   _____

6. How do you think your problem can be solved?

   _____

   _____

7. Is your organization committed to solving the problem?

   _____

   _____

8. Is your organization ready to implement suggested changes?

   _____

   _____

9. Who will my designated liaison be on this project?

   _____

   _____

10. When is the latest you would like to have this project completed?

    _____

    _____

20 Questions, continued

11. When is the earliest you would like to have this project completed?

_____

_____

12. What will your role be during the project?

_____

_____

13. Will you supply me with all the data I request?

_____

_____

14. Have you developed a budget to pay for the changes I recommend?

_____

_____

15. How much have you budgeted to pay for a consultant?

_____

_____

16 Are there any confidential or restricted documents I will be working with?

_____

_____

17. How often can we meet?

_____

_____

18. Can meetings be called as necessary?

_____

_____

19. How often would you like progress reports?

_____

_____

20. When would you like me to begin?

_____

_____

By the time you have asked your clients these 20 questions (and recorded their answers), you will have all the information you need to draft your contract or simple letter of agreement.

Sample Consulting Report

Fort Delaware Society Fundraising Report

After carefully studying the Fort Delaware Society's position as a nonprofit agency in the State of Delaware, the following fundraising plan has been drafted for your review. It is recommended that the board of directors carefully review each item, and decide if, and when, it would like to proceed.

Although no fundraising plan is even guaranteed or foolproof, this one has been designed to raise $26 million for the Fort Delaware Society over the next three years.

1. Private Foundation Support: $24 million

Delaware's largest foundations include: Longwood, Welfare, Laffey-McHugh, Marmot, Crystal Trust, Delaware Community Foundation, Sharp Foundation, Beneficial Foundation, and Life-Enrichment Foundation. The top foundations—Longwood, Welfare, Marmot, Laffey-McHugh, and Crystal Trust—should be solicited for a total of $3 million a year over three years. The remaining Delaware foundations should be solicited for a total of $1 million per year over three years (total: $12 million).

Other foundations that have a history of funding projects like the renovation and restoration of Fort Delaware include: Pew Charitable Trusts, AT&T Foundation, Fidelity Foundation, Chrysler Foundation, Merrill Lynch Foundation, Abell Foundation, Newman's Own Foundation, F.M. Kirby Foundation, Allegheny Foundation, Cafritz Foundation, Andrew Mellon Foundation, Stern Foundation, Wray Trust, Heinz Endowments, J. Paul Getty Trust, and the Turner Foundation. There are dozens of others, but these should be contacted first. Collectively, you should request $4 million per year over three years (total: $12 million).

Note: Fort Delaware Society also qualifies to request money from additional foundations that participate in the National Standard Grant Application. These foundations have joined together to make the application process simple. Once a master application has been received, an agency can make copies and send them in to the appropriate foundations on the list. After carefully reviewing the list, it looks as if Fort Delaware Society has an additional opportunity to solicit 70 foundations. Amounts range from $25,000 to $2 million.

Sample Consulting Report, continued

Recommendation: Beginning in November, start soliciting funds from the Delaware foundations, the national foundations, and the foundations on the National Standard Grant Application list.

2. Corporate and Business Support: $1.75 million

Partnerships between nonprofit agencies and businesses are slowly beginning to mature and take important directions. While it is the normal procedure to solicit a corporation or small business for a contribution, it is suggested that Fort Delaware Society set itself apart from the other nonprofits that are constantly sending letters asking for "just a handout." Instead, Fort Delaware Society should devise a program known as the "Adopt the Fort" plan. This plan consists of asking corporations and small businesses to "adopt" a section of the Fort. The "adoption" process not only involves their contributing money, but also providing volunteers and in-kind donations. (For example, suppose First USA Bank adopts the Fort for one year. It may donate $20,000 and supply volunteers from its employee committees. Companies may also contribute other items on your wish list, as needed. They would also be in a position to host a picnic for their employees at the Fort, thereby increasing the number of visitors and increasing Fort Delaware Society's mailing list.)

These types of "adoption" plans have been successful with schools and businesses throughout the country. Very few other nonprofit agencies have yet to try this approach; Fort Delaware Society has an opportunity to be on the cutting edge and lead the way in Delaware with a new approach to corporate and business giving.

Recommendation: Beginning in January, start soliciting the top 500 corporations and small businesses in New Castle County to participate in the "Adopt the Fort" plan. (I have the list of the 500 top corporations and businesses.)

Important Note: Random surveys were taken during the past 90 days, and, unfortunately, out of 1,000 people surveyed, only 167 had ever heard about Fort Delaware or Pea Patch Island. By going forward with the "Adopt the Fort" plan, hundreds of thousands of Delawareans would be exposed to the Fort.

3. Special Events: $150,000

A "Walk For The Fort" event should be held in the fall (mid to late September). Because of the uniqueness of Pea Patch Island and the Fort, this type of walkathon

Sample Consulting Report, continued

should attract approximately 1,000 walkers. Each walker would be required to raise a minimum of $100 to qualify for an incentive prize (T-shirt, sport bottle, etc., with the Fort Delaware logo and logo of the corporate sponsor that provides the prize). Additional money can be raised through other sponsorship opportunities (signage, refreshments, entertainment, etc.). This day long event will again raise greater awareness of the Fort to the general public.

Recommendation: For this event to be a success, a walk committee should be formed no later than January 15. I can provide an entire how-to kit, which lists the steps necessary to hold a successful walkathon.

4. Miscellaneous: $100,000

Other ways to generate fundraising dollars include:

○ *Direct mail.* Using both the current Fort Delaware Society mailing list and a new prospect list, solicit for funds with a two-page letter and an information sheet about the Fort. (Start this campaign in March; I will supply a new prospect list.)

○ *Sponsorships and advertising.* Offer corporations an opportunity to advertise at the Fort when it is open. Many businesses would be willing to pay top dollar to have their signs, banners, etc., at such a unique location. This is fairly easy to implement: Simply contact advertising agencies in the tri-state area, and they will take care of selling the idea to their clients.

○ *Sale of pieces of property.* (On paper only, of course!) Just in time for the holidays, people will be able to give a unique gift to their loved ones. No more fruit-cakes, ties, slippers, etc. Instead, for only $25, they can "buy" a certificate (printed on old-time parchment paper, to look like it has been around awhile) that says they own a "piece of property." This has worked well with people who "buy" stars out of the sky and receive only a certificate with their name on it! The pieces of property could be sold in a variety of ways: at the mall; from your web site; on QVC (home shopping network, always looking for something "dif-ferent"); or at selected gift and novelty shops in the area. You could even market them through schools and nonprofit agencies and offer them the opportunity to make $5 on each certificate they sell. You would receive less money but would make up the difference in volume.

Sample Consulting Update Report

By mid-September, the research for your Capital Improvement Campaign should be completed. The research will be divided into several categories: Foundations (Delaware, regional, and national), Corporations, and Small Businesses. In addition, we will explore the possibility of holding a major special event next year.

Delaware Foundations: The following foundations in Delaware accept requests for contributions from qualified 501(c)3 organizations.

	Average Grant Amount
Beneficial Foundation Inc.	$25,000
Bernard A. & Rebecca S. Bernard Foundation	$20,000
Chichester duPont Foundation Inc.	$35,000
Crestlea Foundation	$25,000
Crystal Trust	$40,000
Delaware Community Foundation	$10,000
Ederic Foundation	$50,000
Fair Play Foundation	$30,000
Good Samaritan Inc.	$15,000
Kent-Lucas Foundation	$15,000
Milton & Hattie Kutz Foundation	$10,000
Laffey-McHugh Foundation	$50,000
Longwood Foundation	$250,000
Life-Enrichment Foundation	$15,000
Lovett Foundation	$15,000
Marmot Foundation	$50,000
Sharp Foundation	$35,000
Welfare Foundation	$75,000

It is strongly suggested that the Possum Point Players submit a request to each of the above foundations for a capital grant. Over the course of the next several weeks, I will prepare additional detailed information concerning the address, deadlines, and what information is required for each application.

Recommendations for the next 30 to 45 days:

○ Continue researching other sources of foundation funds. (John Doe)

○ Start compiling your mailing list and make sure it includes vendors, present and past contributors, and patrons. Also, have all board members start making lists of people they know (business contacts, relatives, friends, church acquaintances, etc.). These lists will be added to a database of people who can be solicited for a donation. (Board)

○ Develop several special event ideas. (John Doe) . . . .

○ Develop a list of noncapital funding resources. (John Doe)

Appendix
Consulting Service Resources

They say you can never be too rich or too thin. Although these could be argued, we believe "You can never have too many resources." Therefore, we present for your consideration a wealth of sources for you to check into, check out, and harness for your own personal information blitz. These sources are tidbits, ideas to get you started on your research.

They are by no means the only sources out there, and they should not be taken as the Ultimate Answer. We have done our research, but businesses—like customers—tend to move, change, fold, and expand. As we have repeatedly stressed, do your homework. Get out and start investigating.

Books

The Business of Consulting: The Basics and Beyond, Elaine Biech, Pfeiffer

The Consultant's Calling: Bringing Who You Are to What You Do, Geoffrey M. Bellman, Jossey-Bass

Flawless Consulting: A Guide to Getting Your Expertise Used, Peter Block, Pfeiffer

How to Succeed as an Independent Consultant, Herman Holtz and David Zahn, John Wiley & Sons

Marketing Your Services: A Step-by-Step Guide for Small Businesses and Professionals, Anthony O. Putman, John Wiley & Sons

Million Dollar Consulting: The Professional's Guide to Growing a Practice, Alan Weiss, McGraw-Hill

The Skilled Facilitator, Roger Schwarz, Jossey-Bass

Business Software

Dreamweaver MX, Macromedia Inc., 600 Townsend St., San Francisco, CA 94103, (800) 470-7211, (415) 252-2000, fax: (415) 626-0554, www.macromedia.com

Microsoft Office, available from most computer and office supply stores, including Comp USA (www.compusa.com), and Office Depot (www.officedepot.com)

QuickBooks Basic, Intuit Inc., (888) 246-8848, www.quickbooks.com

Peachtree, Best Software Inc., 1505 Pavilion Pl., Norcross, GA 30093, (770) 724-4000, www.peachtree.com

Consultants

Jeffery Bartlett, The Bartlett Group, 3690 Vartan Way, Harrisburg, PA 17110

Susan Bock, Susan Bock Solutions, 8201 Newman Ave., #102, Huntington Beach, CA 92647, (714) 847-1566, fax: (714) 847-5715, www.susanbocksolutions.com, e-mail: susan@sbocksolutions.com

David P. McMullen, McMullen Consulting, P.O. Box 10443, Costa Mesa, CA 92627, (714) 948-8905, fax: (714) 948-8905, www.mcmullenconsulting.com, e-mail: dave@mcmullenconsulting.com

Bill Metten, Bill Metten and Associates, 21 Stuyvesant Dr., Hockessin, DE 09707, (302) 234-9936, e-mail: billm@delanet.com

Melinda Patrician, 4229 S. 36th St., Arlington, VA 22206, (703) 824-1765

Merrily Schiavone, AdHelp Inc., 50 Millwright Dr., Newark, DE 19711, (302) 366-0681, www.adhelp.us

Consulting Organizations

American Association of Healthcare Consultants, 5938 N. Drake Ave., Chicago, IL 60659, (888) 350-2242, fax: (773) 463-3552, www.aahc.net, e-mail: info@aahcmail.org

American Consultants League, c/o ETR, 245 NE Fourth Ave., #102, Delray Beach, FL 33483, (866) 344-7200, www.americanconsultantsleague.com

Association of Management Consulting Firms, 380 Lexington Ave., #1700, New York, NY 10168, (212) 551-7887, fax: (212) 551-7934, www.amcf.org, e-mail: info@amcf.org

Association of Professional Communication Consultants, www.consultingsuccess.org

Association of Professional Consultants, P.O. Box 51193, Irvine, CA 92619-1193, (800) 745-5050, fax: (800) 977-3272, www.consultapc.org, e-mail: apc@consultapc.org

Canadian Association of Management Consultants, BCE Pl., 181 Bay St., Heritage Building Fl. 2R, Toronto, ON, CAN M5J 2T3, (416) 860-1515, (800) 268-1148, fax: (416) 860-1535, (800) 662-2972, www.camc.com, e-mail: consulting@camc.com

Institute of Management Consultants, 2025 M St. NW, #800, Washington, DC 20036-3309, (202) 367-2134, (800) 221-2557, fax: (202) 367-2134, www.imcusa.org

National Association of Computer Consultant Businesses, 1420 King St., #610, Alexandria, VA 22314, (703) 838-2050, fax: (703) 838-3610, www.naccb.org, e-mail: staff@naccb.org

Professional and Technical Consultants Association, 543 Vista Mar Ave., Pacifica, CA 94044, (408) 971-5902, (800) 74-PATCA, fax: (650) 359-3089, www.patca.org, e-mail: info@patca.org

Public Relations Society of America, 33 Maiden Ln., 11th Fl., New York, NY 10038-5150, (212) 460-1400, fax: (212) 995-0757, www.prsa.org

Society of Professional Consultants, P.O. Box 785, Westford, MA 01886, (978) 692-6950, fax: (987) 692-7672 www.spconsultants.org

Consulting Publications

Consultants News, Kennedy Information Inc., 1 Phoenix Mill Ln., Fl. 5, Peterborough, NH 03458, (800) 531-0007, www.consultingcentral.com

Consulting Magazine, Kennedy Information Inc., 1 Phoenix Mill Ln., Fl. 5, Peterborough, NH 03458, (800) 531-0007, www.consultingmag.com, ckrunklevich@kennedyinfo.com

Consulting Success, www.consultingsuccess.org

Consulting to Management, 858 Longview Rd., Burlingame, CA 94010-6974, (650) 342-1954, fax: (650) 344-5005, www.c2m.com

ConsultingWire, Kennedy Information Inc., http://register.consultingcentral.com

Inside Consulting, Consulting Information Services LLC, 191 Washington St., Keene, NH 03431, (603) 355-1560, www.consultinginfo.com, e-mail: tom.roden hauser@consultinginfo.com

Education/Training/Certification Resources

AAPC Division/American Association of Professional Consultants, c/o National Bureau of Certified, Consultants Inc., 1850 Fifth Ave., San Diego, CA 92101, (619) 239-7076, (800) 543-1114, fax: (619) 296-3580, www.national-bureau.org, e-mail: national bureau@att.net

American Consultants League, c/o ETR, 345 NE Fourth Ave., #102, Delray Beach, FL 33483, (866) 344-7200, wwsw.americanconsultantsleague.com

Century University, 6400 Uptown Blvd. NE, Albuquerque, NM 87110, (800) 240-6757 www.centuryuniversity.edu

Institute of Management Consultants USA, 2025 M St. NW, #800, Washington, DC 20036-3309, (202) 367-2134, (800) 221-2557, fax: (202) 367-2134, www.imcusa.org

National Bureau of Certified Consultants Inc., 1850 Fifth Ave., San Diego, CA 92101, (619) 239-7076, (800) 543-1114, fax: (619) 296-3580, www.national-bureau.org, e-mail: nationalbureau@att.net

San Diego State University, College of Extended Studies, 5250 Campanile Dr., San Diego, CA 92182-1925, (619) 594-5821, fax: (619) 594-8566, www.ces.sdsu.edu, e-mail: extended.std@sdsu.edu

University of Georgia Center for Continuing Education, 1197 South Lumpkin St., Athens, GA 30602-3603, (800) 488-7827 (press Option 3), fax: (706) 542-2635, e-mail: certificate.programs@gactr.uga.edu

Government Agencies

Minority Business Development Agency, 1401 Constitution Ave. NW, Washington, DC 20230, (888) 324-1551, www.mbda.gov, e-mail: help@mbda.gov

U.S. Department of Labor, Frances Perkins Bldg., 200 Constitution Ave. NW, Washington, DC 20210, (866) 4-USA-DOL, www.dol.gov

Incorporation Kits

Inc. Plan USA, Trolley Square, Suite 26c, Wilmington, DE 19806, (302) 428-1200, (800) 462-4633, fax: (302) 428-1274, www.incplan.net

Quality Books, 315 SW 50th St., Miami, FL 33134, (786) 552-5042, fax: (800) 887-6123 www.qualitybooks.com, e-mail: customerservice@qualitybooks. com

Skyweb Enterprises, 3023 Wakefield Dr., Ste. I, Carpentersville, IL 60110, (847) 836-7399, fax: (847) 836-7397 www.primeprofits.com, e-mail: webmaster@primeprofits.com

Office Supplies, Forms, and Stationery

Amsterdam Printing, 166 Wallins Corner Rd., Amsterdam, NY 12010, (800) 833-6231, fax: (518) 843-5204, www.amsterdamprinting.com

Office Depot, www.officedepot.com

Office Max, www.officemax.com

Paper Direct Internet, 1025 East Woodmen Rd., Colorado Springs, CO 80920, (800) A-PAPERS, fax: (800) 443-2973, www.paperdirect.com, e-mail: customerservice@ paperdirect.com

Rapidforms, 301 Grove Rd., Thorofare, NJ 08086, (800) 257-5287, fax: (800) 451-8113, www.rapidforms.com, e-mail: service@rapidforms.com

Staples, www.staples.com

Pagers

Beepers.com, 96 Oak Ridge Rd., Oak Ridge, NJ 07438, (800) BEEPERS, www.beepers.com, e-mail: info@beepers.com

Printing Resources

ColorPrintingCentral, (800) 309-3291, www.colorprintingcentral.com

Print Industry Exchange LLC, P.O. Box 2238, Ashburn, VA 20146-2238, (703) 631-4533, fax: (703) 729-2268, www.printindustry.com, e-mail: info@printindustry.com

Printing for Less, 211 E. Geyser St., Livingston, MT 59047, (800) 930-6040, (406) 222-2689, www.printingforless.com, e-mail: info@printingforless.com

Print Quote USA, 23012B Oxford Pl., Boca Raton, FL 33433, (561) 451-2654, fax: (561) 725-0246, www.printquoteusa.com

Promotion Xpress, 2096 Merced St., San Leandro, CA 94577, (888) 310-7769, (510) 357-0238, fax: (510) 357-2088, www.proxprint.com, e-mail: support@proxprint.com

PSPrint, 2861 Mandela Pkwy., Oakland, CA 94608, (800) 511-2009, (510) 444-3933, fax: (510) 444-5369, www.psprint.com

Telecom Companies

AT&T Small and Medium Business, (800) 222-0400, www.att.com/business

Carolinanet, (888) 400-5557, https://carolinanet.nuvio.com/index02.php

Hello Direct, 75 Northeastern Blvd., Nashua, NH 03062, (800) 435-5634, www.hellodirect.com

Sage Telecom, 805 Central Expwy. S., #100, Allen, TX 75013, (888) 226-2121, www.sagetelecom.net

Web Hosting/Domain Names

Apollo Hosting, 2303 Ranch Rd. 620 South, #135-301, Austin, TX 78734, (877) 525-HOST, (512) 261-1203, fax: (800) 861-0986, www.apollohosting.com

Domain.com, (800) 583-3382, www.domain.com

EarthLink, (800) 324-8454, www.earthlink.net

iPowerWeb, 2800 28th St., #205, Santa Monica, CA 90405, (888) 511-HOST, www.ipowerweb.com, e-mail: sales@ipowerweb.com

NetPass, 419 N. Magnolia Ave., Orlando, FL 32801, (407) 843-7277, fax: (407) 843-2105, www.netpass.com, e-mail: support@netpass.com

Web Hosting, g.com, (888) WEBHOST, www.webhosting.com, e-mail: sales@web-hosting.com

Yahoo!, (866) 781-9246, http://smallbusiness.yahoo.com

Glossary

Corporation: a form of business ownership that protects the owner's personal assets against potential business losses.

DBA: acronym for "doing business as" that refers to any name chosen as a business name, including those that include the owner's name (as in David Jones and Associates).

Domain name: the address of an internet network (for example, www.entrepreneur.com); also known as the URL.

DSL line: acronym for Digital Subscriber Line, a type of technology that provides high-speed access to the internet.

Electronic business card: little more than a "place marker" on the internet meant to provide basic information such as business name, address and phone number.

Ergonomic: scientifically designed for the comfort and safety of the people who use them (for example, an ergonomic chair).

Flash: an electronic file format used on a web page that consists of graphics and/or animation; also known as Shockwave Flash.

Footprint: the amount of space something (typically electronic equipment) occupies.

Home page: the electronic gateway to your internet web site.

ISP: Internet Service Provider.

Lead: the opening line of an article or news release; should be written to announce the most important thing you want the reader to know.

Link: an electronic connection on your web site that when clicked opens pages elsewhere on the site or on another web site.

LLC: Limited Liability Company, a type of legal business entity.

News release: a one-to-two-page article, often on company letterhead, used to generate favorable publicity; also known as a press release.

Partnership: a business owned by two or more persons, or partners, in equal or unequal proportions.

Resolution: the clarity of a computer printer or monitor, expressed as dpi (dots per inch).

Sole proprietorship: a business owned by one person.

Unsecured personal loan: a loan that doesn't require collateral.

URL: Uniform Resource Locator, or the internet address locator of a web site.

Index